Charlemagne's Months and their Bavarian Labors

The politics of the Seasons in the Carolingian Empire

Carl I. Hammer

BAR International Series 676
1997

Published in 2019 by
BAR Publishing, Oxford

BAR International Series 676

Charlemagne's Months and their Bavarian Labors

© Carl I. Hammer and the Publisher 1997

The author's moral rights under the 1988 UK Copyright,
Designs and Patents Act are hereby expressly asserted.

All rights reserved. No part of this work may be copied, reproduced, stored,
sold, distributed, scanned, saved in any form of digital format or transmitted
in any form digitally, without the written permission of the Publisher.

ISBN 9780860548652 paperback
ISBN 9781407349879 e-book

DOI https://doi.org/10.30861/9780860548652

A catalogue record for this book is available from the British Library

This book is available at www.barpublishing.com

BAR Publishing is the trading name of British Archaeological Reports (Oxford) Ltd.
British Archaeological Reports was first incorporated in 1974 to publish the BAR
Series, International and British. In 1992 Hadrian Books Ltd became part of the BAR
group. This volume was originally published by Archaeopress in conjunction with
British Archaeological Reports (Oxford) Ltd / Hadrian Books Ltd, the Series principal
publisher, in 1997. This present volume is published by BAR Publishing, 2019.

BAR
PUBLISHING

BAR titles are available from:

        BAR Publishing
        122 Banbury Rd, Oxford, OX2 7BP, UK
EMAIL   info@barpublishing.com
PHONE +44 (0)1865 310431
FAX   +44 (0)1865 316916
        www.barpublishing.com

TABLE of CONTENTS

	Page
Appended Exhibits and List of Plates	ii
Preface and Acknowledgments	iii

I. Seasonal Texts and Images

Introduction	1
A. The *Libri Carolini*	2
B. Classical Literary and Artistic Traditions of the Seasons and the Months	6
C. Charlemagne's Months	8
D. The Labors of the Months	14
E. Comparisons and Perspectives	25
F. Some Interim Art-Historical Conclusions	27

II. Political Contexts and Personalities

A. The Carolingian Reconstruction of Bavaria	31
B. Archbishop Arn of Salzburg	32
C. Sheriff Audulf in Bavaria	33
D. Audulf and Court Culture	41
E. Archbishop Hildebald and Bishop Baturich	43
F. Carolingian Claims and Agilolfing Echoes	46
Concluding Observations	51

Appendix: Wandalbert of Prüm on the Months	53
Bibliography and Addendum	71

TABLE of CONTENTS

Appended Exhibits

Sketch Map: Carolingian Bavaria and the Province of Salzburg

Schematic Figure: Three-Field System of Cultivation

Exhibit: Typology of Seasonal Representations

Table 1: Comparison of Classical and Medieval Labors of the Months

Table 2: Summary of Correspondences to the Salzburg Labors

List of Plates and Sources (see also "Bibliography")

1. **Color Frontispiece: The Salzburg "Labors of the Months" in Vienna, National Library, Codex 387, fo.90v**, from D.Bullough, *The Age of Charlemagne*, Paul Elek Ltd, London, 1973, Pl.58, p.144.

2. **Representations of February, March, August and September in the Codex-Calendar of 354, Bibliothèque Royale, Brussels**, MS 7543-7549, fo.201r, from M.R.Salzman, *On Roman Time*, University of California Press, Berkeley/Los Angeles/Oxford, 1990, Fig.49.

3. **Representations of the Four Seasons and the Twelve months from the El Djem mosaic, Tunisia**, Musée Archéologique, from D.Parrish, *Season Mosaics of Roman North Africa*, Giorgio Bretschneider Editore, Rome, 1984, Pl.42.

4. **Representations of "The Labors of the Months" in Vienna, National Library, Codex 387, fo.90v, and Munich, State Library, Clm 210, fo.91v**, from G.Swarzenski, *Die Salzburger Malerei*, Verlag von Karl W. Hiersemann, Leipzig, 1908, Tafelband, Abb.20/21.

5. **Representations of the Winds in Vienna, National Library, Codex 387, fo.140r, and Munich, State Library, Clm 210, fo.139r**, from G.Swarzenski, *Die Salzburger Malerei*, Tafelband, Abb.22/23.

6. **Representation of Jupiter in the 11th-century Montecassino Manuscript of Hrabanus Maurus' *Encyclopedia***, from *Miniature sacre e profane dell'anno 1023*, Tipo-Litografia di Montecassino, 1896, Pl.CVIII.

7. **Representations of the Twelve Months in the Martyrology of Wandalbert of Prüm, Vatican Library, Rome**, MS Reg.lat.438, from J.C.Webster, *The Labors of the Months*, Princeton University Press, Princeton, 1938, Pl.XI.

PREFACE and ACKNOWLEDGMENTS

For almost 20 years my research, whenever I could spare time from business duties, has concentrated on the social and demographic history of early-medieval Bavaria, particularly on the condition of the servile groups which formed by far the largest part of that society. Like most medievalists I thought that we possessed at least one authentic representation of those obscure, but certainly not anonymous, people, preserved in a pair of calendrical manuscripts produced in the early ninth century. These are the well-known Salzburg "Labors of the Months" (Plate 1: Frontispiece). My original intention for this paper was very limited: to explain an apparent anomaly in the representation of the month April. But, as I worked on that smaller question, I was drawn ever further into a larger and more intractable set of problems. I finally concluded, very unwillingly, that these pictures were really about something quite different. This study is my attempt to indicate what that might be.

Work of this nature necessarily involved me in a number of new areas such as art history, and, consequently, I have a much larger-than-usual number of obligations to acknowledge. The art-historical research benefited from the outstanding research collection and the congenial surroundings of the Frick Fine Arts Library at the University of Pittsburgh, and the medievalists on the faculty there, Professors Fil Hearn, Alison Stones, Frank Toker and John Williams, gave me the first opportunities to discuss my work and to present it to a larger audience. The German Academic Exchange Service (DAAD) provided a timely research grant to spend one month during January and February 1996 in Munich which allowed me to consult historical works not available in Pittsburgh and to examine the two manuscripts which are the focus of this essay. In this regard, I want to thank particularly Professor Horst Fuhrmann, President of the Bavarian Academy of Sciences and former President of the *Monumenta Germaniae Historica*, and Professor Wilhelm Störmer, now retired from the Institute for Bavarian History, Munich, for their kindness and support over many years as well as for their scholarly comments. I also want to recognize especially the continuing encouragement and hospitality of Professor Michael Mitterauer, the head of the Institute for Economic and Social History at the University of Vienna.

Professor Rudolf Schieffer and Professor Walter Ziegler, the libraries and staffs of their respective institutions, the *Monumenta Germaniae Historica* and the Institute for Bavarian History, provided ideal scholarly conditions for my work in Munich. Professor Schieffer also read a draft of the essay and generously discussed it with me. Dr Dieter Kudorfer (coincidentally, a dormitory mate from my first stay in Munich in 1963/4!) and the staff of the Manuscript Section of the Bavarian State Library, Munich, made their valuable illuminated manuscript, Clm 210, and related items available to me for detailed examination. The staff of the Manuscript and Incunabula Collection of the Austrian National Library provided friendly and efficient access to Codex 387 which I had to consult on a very tight schedule while on a one-day visit to Vienna; Dr Eva Irblich of that library provided additional information and help. Finally, in Munich Dr Gertrud Diepolder and Professor Kurt Reindel both read the draft of this essay and made valuable comments. From Cambridge Dr Rosamond McKitterick also provided welcome advice, and Professor Dennis Looney of the University of Pittsburgh saved me from several slips and infelicities in my translation of Wandalbert of Prüm's remarkable poem.

In view of such generous assistance to a person with no fixed academic address, it is particularly important for me to emphasize that all of the above are completely free of any complicity in or responsibility for my excesses or errors which certainly remain despite their best efforts.

I. SEASONAL TEXTS AND IMAGES

INTRODUCTION

In the 1889 "Communications" of the Institute for Austrian Historical Research, the distinguished art historian, Alois Riegl, published an article on medieval calendar illustrations which has set the direction for much subsequent research.[1] However, Riegl apparently was unaware of his country's most significant contribution to the medieval development of this *genre*, the two early-ninth-century illustrations of the "Labors of the Months" produced in the area of Salzburg (Plates 1 [Frontispiece] and 4).[2] They are the earliest explicitly *calendrical* illustrations this important pictorial tradition which would become an immense vogue in the twelfth century and persist in popularity to the end of the medieval period and beyond.

These pictures are incorporated into two very large, contemporary manuscripts of identical composition containing, primarily, collections of treatises on astronomical and calendrical calculations (the so-called *computus*). Both manuscripts were produced in the vicinity of Salzburg. The artistically more accomplished of the two is now held in the Austrian National Library in Vienna (Codex 387).[3] The second manuscript is at the Bavarian State Library in Munich (Clm 210). A surviving doublet of such ambitious (and expensive) manuscripts is, itself, extraordinary and deserves comment, since their production implies some sort of normative intent. But, until very recently, with the revived interest in the tradition of the medieval *computus*, these two manuscripts were known almost exclusively for the single folio page in each which contains the earliest medieval depiction of the "Labors of the Months" and which has been reproduced in numerous secondary works as an illustration of early-medieval peasant life.[4]

This essay has two objectives. In the first section, "Seasonal Texts and Images", I will examine the illustrations of the "Labors" and their manuscripts from the perspectives of art and intellectual history in order to place these pictures within the context of contemporary, Carolingian cultural life and, then, attempt to determine whether the pictures are, indeed, original depictions of contemporary rural life or, perhaps, something more complex. In the second section, "Political Contexts and Personalities", I shall try to place the pictures within a more conventional historical context and suggest why the manuscripts were produced precisely when and where they

---

[1] "Mittelalterliche Kalenderillustration".

[2] Nevertheless, he did suspect, correctly, a picture cycle behind the related Salzburg poems, the *Carmina Salisburgensia*, that he analyzed, *ibid.*, p.38.

[3] See below, Section I.D. for a detailed discussion of these manuscripts and their contents.

[4] For a recent example, see the excellent catalogue of the joint Bavarian-Salzburg exhibition, *Die Bajuwaren*, Plates 106, 122-4, 126, which describes the pictures as "representations of provincial peasant agriculture (*Darstellungen des bäuerlichen Wirtschaftslebens*)", p.167.

were, who were their sponsors, and what was their programmatic intent. Both of these discussions will require the consideration of a number of (apparently) diverse issues and will remain, necessarily, circumstantial in their argument. But, I believe, they will demonstrate that the long-prevailing unreflective and naive view of these pictures is fundamentally wrong. Moreover, I hope that the following discussion will have the additional merit of introducing a group of remarkable personalities who shaped both the cultural and political life of Carolingian Bavaria and whose achievements are too little known and appreciated. Our modern view of the Seasons, even their conventional number (4), and the progress of the Months has been conditioned by a long and complex cultural tradition which has subtly formed our appreciation of their natural features. As we shall see, many of the fundamental characteristics of this view were fixed in Classical Antiquity, but these Salzburg pictures are an important part of the medieval filter through which it was both transmitted and reshaped, since (as I shall argue) they appropriate the past in order to transform their present.

A. The *Libri Carolini*

Between 790 and 792 an international team of scholars associated with Charlemagne's Court composed a unique theological work combining vigorous polemics with immense learning. Because there is reason to think that Charlemagne himself took a direct interest and participated to some extent in its preparation, the four-part volume is conventionally referred to as the *Libri Carolini* or, "Carl's Books". The primary author undoubtedly was Theodulf, Bishop of Orléans.[5] The purpose of the work was to refute the supposedly inflated and heretical claims made for the importance of holy pictures (icons) by the Eastern Church at the Council of Nicea II which concluded in 787. However, any purely scholarly ambitions and interests were undermined by a string of misunderstandings and mistranslations, poor communications, suspicions between East and West, and the tentative and exploratory relationship then existing between the Frankish King and the Roman Pope. In the end, the book was seen to be inappropriate to the situation and was committed to the archives. It was a dead letter.

Nevertheless, it remains of considerable interest to modern scholars as one of the major intellectual statements of the period, revealing, often indirectly, the preoccupations of the King and his intellectuals on a variety of issues. One of these certainly was a "Christian-imperial" claim for the legitimacy of Frankish rulership against Byzantium.[6] Another, related concern was the role of the visual arts in the religious cult and, indeed, the whole function of art within the emerging medieval society of Northern Europe, particularly its relation to Classical traditions of visual representation. This confrontation is addressed concisely in the *Libri Carolini's* Third Book at the 23rd Chapter. In fact, this section is unique within the entire work, for it is the one place where, "it touches upon the

---

[5]) Freeman, "Carolingian Orthodoxy". For the possible influence of the great Anglo-Saxon scholar, Alcuin *cf.* the essays by Wallach, *Diplomatic Studies*.

[6]) Noble, "Tradition and Learning", pp.246-8.

I. Seasonal Texts and Images

power of images to illustrate and thus to teach".[7]

The point of departure was the primacy of the Word over the Picture. Its pretext: visual representations must derive their authority from Scripture or, presumably, from some other acceptable source in verbal culture. The subtext, however, was the dubious heritage of Classical paganism with its perceived hedonism and its personification of powers in both the natural and the supernatural worlds. The author of the *Libri Carolini* asserted that the Eastern Church began with the claim, "Painters do not contradict the Scriptures". However, the *Libri Carolini* then pointed out that many subjects are depicted in paintings regarding which the Holy Scriptures are silent and which, moreover, are understood to be in serious error, not only by the learned but even by the uneducated. Therefore, the writer concludes, "Who would not admit that this [Eastern] position is both completely ridiculous and false!" In fact, this passage adduces many specific examples to illustrate the argument such as personifications of natural processes and elements, or rivers, or the sun, the moon, and the stars. This short section of the *Libri Carolini* then concludes with a complex diatribe which widens out from representations of forces in the natural world to the broader context of natural time and human activity.

"Is it not, likewise, evident that those artists contradict Holy Scripture--in which these things are scarcely contained--when they attribute particular forms to each of the twelve winds according to their powers; or who give human shape to each of the months according to the character of the season, whatever each of them brings forth, some of them completely naked, others half naked, still others arrayed in various costumes; or who depict the four seasons of the year each in an individual human form: either verdant with flowers as Spring; or dried up by the heat or weighed down with crops as Summer; or burdened with the vats and grape clusters of the vintage as Autumn; or sometimes freezing with cold, sometimes warming himself by the fire, sometimes offering fodder to the beasts, sometimes capturing birds enfeebled by excessive cold as Winter."[8]

Did Theodulf, the author of the *Libri Carolini*, have any particular works in mind as the basis for his very specific examples? The emblems of the four seasons clearly incorporate much conventional seasonal iconography from Classical Antiquity, best preserved for us in a number of surviving friezes, murals and, especially, mosaics as well as in poetry.[9] The figures of the months,

---

[7]) Freeman, "Scripture and Images", p.174. I have not been able to consult H.Schade, "Die Libri Carolini und ihre Stellung zum Bild", *Zeitschrift für katholische Theologie*, vol.86, (1957).

[8]) *Libri Carolini*, pp.150-1 (my translation). Dr W.Setz of the MGH kindly provided me with relevant printouts of Dr Freeman's new edition which he is preparing for publication. The entire Chapter is translated in Davis-Weyer, *Early Medieval Art*, pp.100-3.

[9]) For the Classical and early-medieval traditions see the fundamental discussions in: Webster,

however, recall specifically the great and unique Codex-Calendar of the year 354 which was prepared by the famous calligrapher, Filocalus, for the aristocratic Roman Christian, Valentinus.[10]

This important work was the object of at least two ninth-century copies: the illustrated but now-lost "Luxemburgensis" which, apparently, was copied from the original and which survives in several 15th- and 16th-century copies, and the unillustrated "Sangallensis" manuscript.[11] Two copies of such an elaborate (and expensive) work certainly witness to a lively, contemporary interest in the fully-developed Roman calendrical tradition which it represents where the individual months, in the Classical tradition, are personified with certain appropriate attributes, e.g. a flower or a sheaf of grain. And, indeed, the personifications of the summer and early-autumn months are "completely naked" (June-October), March could be called "half naked" and the rest are "arrayed in various costumes" (Plate 2). Even if Filocalus' calendar (original or copy) was not the specific source of this reference (and we shall see presently that the Codex-Calendar was not without contemporary influence), the author of the *Libri Carolini* must have had something very similar in mind.[12]

From this perspective, Theodulf's alarm is more comprehensible. No doubt, there is a bit of prudishness here which may surprise us in a work associated with Charlemagne who enjoyed communal bathing, had numerous concubines, and who maintained a distinctly odd relationship with his daughters.[13] Nevertheless, prudery combined with the prurient is not unknown, and, on this point, Riegl remarked somewhat tartly that only the limited mental horizons of the more general Carolingian audience determined that, "regarding the qualities of the offensive representations of the months, only the parallel between the temperature of the respective month and the extent of the clothing", was noted explicitly.[14] Surely, however, it was also the specifically pagan connotations of the Roman calendrical tradition which were cause for intellectual and spiritual concern. Even in a work produced for the Christian Valentinus we find a thorough integration of zodiacal lore and pagan cult transmitted through the annual

---

Labors of the Months; Hanfmann, *Season Sarcophagus*; Stern, "Les calendriers"; and Comet, "Les calendriers médiévaux". There is a lively discussion of the late-medieval tradition by Henisch: "In Due Season".

[10]) Stern, *Le calendrier de 354*; Salzman, *On Roman Time*.

[11]) Salzman, *On Roman Time*, pp.70-3.

[12]) Riegl, "Mittelalterliche Kalenderillustration", pp.33-4; Stern, *Le calendrier*, pp.35-6; *idem*, "Poésies et représentations", p.152, n.3, p.166.

[13]) Charlemagne's relationship to his daughters has now been placed within an intelligible dynastic context by Rudolf Schieffer, "Karolingische Töchter".

[14]) "...von den Qualitäten jener anstössigen Monatsbilder nur der Parallelismus zwischen der Temperatur der jeweiligen Monate und dem Grade der Bekleidung", "Mittelalterliche Kalendarillustration", pp.33-4.

I. Seasonal Texts and Images

cycle of Roman religious and civic festivals to which Ovid's incomplete *Fasti* are a remarkable literary witness. Such syncretism probably appeared natural and acceptable to an educated Roman of the mid-fourth century. But with the still somewhat rustic natives of the North, who, even when cultivated, lacked the easy familiarity derived from everyday associations in classical Rome, it must have brought a type of Frankish Puritanism to the fore.

Moreover, Theodulf brought to this problem a particular sensibility derived from his Visigothic homeland where the hostility of Islam and Judaism to representational art were pervasive influences. In fact (and somewhat surprisingly), we are able to form a very graphic and precise notion of the sort of art which the learned author of the *Libri Carolini* did find acceptable. In the early ninth century, Bishop Theodulf, apparently in imitation of the royal "Pfalz" at Aachen, built an elaborate country residence at Germigny-des-Prés near his episcopal seat of Orléans, and the impressive private chapel (*basilica*) is still extant despite its "restoration".[15] The church, dedicated in early 806, contains both decorative motifs in relief and an elaborate, "restored" mosaic depicting two angels and two immense golden cherubim surrounding the Ark of the Covenant towards which the "right hand of God" (*dextra Dei*) is pointing.[16]

The texts for the mosaics are taken from Exodus (Ch.25) and I Kings (Ch.6). The iconographic aim evidently was to recreate Solomon's temple within the sanctuary space where God is completely hidden to the worshipper.

Peter Bloch remarks that, "Never before or since was God so far removed from any representation in a Western church".[17] Islamic and even Jewish influences are prominent, and the entire scheme, "carr[ies] deliberate undertones of attack on the whole Byzantine position [regarding images]".[18] The most recent reflection on this whole complex of questions is provided by the new editor of the *Libri Carolini* who ascribes that work's obscurity and lack of contemporary influence to the idiosyncracies of the author's, Theodulf's views, which were rooted in a specifically Iberian approach to images with which, "his colleagues at Charlemagne's court...were simply not comfortable". It "remains a very personal and somewhat isolated work".[19]

Yet, it appears that Theodulf's approach to the visual arts may have been more complex than the preceding discussion might suggest. His residence at Germigny may have been the site of the allegorical murals (*picturae*)

---

[15]) Literary descriptions in Schlosser, *Schriftquellen*, Nrs 682, 683, pp.217-8.

[16]) Bloch, "Apsismosaik", pp.234-61; Viellard-Troiekouroff, "Nouvelles études". I have not found any comprehensive treatment of the whole site-complex including the residence.

[17]) "Niemals zuvor und hernach war in einer abendländischen Kirche Gott so fern jeder Gestalt", "Apsismosaik", p.254.

[18]) Dodwell, *Painting in Europe*, p.18; see also Freeman, "Scripture and Images", pp.182-3.

[19]) Freeman, "Scripture and Images", pp.183, 192.

which he describes in two poems on the Seven Liberal Arts and on a map of the world (*imago terrae in modum orbis comprehensa*). The former, on the Liberal Arts, in particular, contains an extended astrological section dealing with the twelve zodiac signs and the seven stars (including the moon) by which "the month, the year and the very day, itself, is governed" (*dirigitur mensis, annus et ipse dies*). Here we are very close to the seasonal themes of calendrical works, and, interestingly, Theodulf legitimates the pagan associations by alluding to their appropriation by Christian culture in Antiquity: "Nor, reader, should the pagan names disturb you, for this venerable usage is allowed by the Fathers [of the Church ?]".[20]

B. Classical Literary and Artistic Traditions of the Seasons and the Months

The Classical tradition of seasonal art attacked in the *Libri Carolini* had a long and complex history. As our Carolingian copies of the Codex-Calendar also bear witness, the notion of depicting the seasons and months appealed to contemporaries, and, indeed, there were complementary strands of the annual cycle's tradition which might provide guidance in avoiding some of the inherent dangers suspected by the *Libri Carolini*. Both approaches derive ultimately from the Greek poet Hesiod's *Works and Days* (ca 700 B.C.), an artful and poetic blend of farmer's calendar, mythological handbook and guide to superstitious practice. The one strand of this tradition, the poetical, is best represented in Virgil's *Georgics*. The other strand, of particular interest to us, is exemplified by the Roman agronomist literature of Cato the Censor (234-149 B.C), Varro (116-27 B.C.), Columella (1st cent.A.D.), and Palladius (4th cent.A.D.).[21]

The Roman agronomists all incorporated some form of calendar arrangement with individual variations and super-/sub-divisions. This principle is quite muted at the beginning in Cato. Both Varro and Columella have extended calendrical sections, incorporating various climatic and astronomical lore, although the strictly topical sections, not the calendrical ones, are the more numerous. The individual months fully dominate the structure of the last writer, Palladius. In addition, we have monumental examples from Italy, roughly contemporary with Columella, of "Country Calendars".[22] These latter are inscribed monuments, but without ornamentation, and list in laconic fashion by month the main agricultural activities along

---

[20]) "Nec tibi displiceant gentilia nomina, lector,/Iste vetustatis mos datur a patribus" (Theodulf, *Carmina*, Nrs 46,47, pp.544-8, esp.p.546 (= Schlosser, *Schriftquellen*, Nrs 1026, 1031). There is a recent, extended discussion of Theodulf in Nees, *Tainted Mantle*, pp.21-143, which contrasts Theodulf's views with Alcuin's on, "the proper relationship between things Christian and things secular, with Theodulf consistently arguing for a sharp separation where Alcuin seemed to be intent upon building bridges" (p.119), although there seems to be a distinction for Theodulf, as in the above passage, between things transmitted from pagan and from Christian Antiquity. See also the statement on the Four Seasons by Bullough, *Age of Charlemagne*, p.189, which I cannot confirm.

[21]) Overview in: Butzer, "Classical Tradition".

[22]) *Menologium Rusticum Colotianum/Vallense*.

with the zodiac sign, the ruling divinity and the principal festivals.

These Roman writers "de re rustica" have exerted remarkable influence reaching down into modern times through the works of the Elizabethan, Thomas Tusser, and onwards, in increasingly literary form, to H.Rider Haggard, Flora Thompson, A.G.Street, and even (on the consumption, not the supply side) to Peter Mayle's *A Year in Province*. But, while Carolingians knew the principal components of this Classical tradition of writing, they did not contribute significantly to it, and it was actively revived only in the later Middle Ages.[23]

In the important, official agricultural "handbook" for the royal estates, the "Capitulare de Villis" from the late-eighth century, the calendrical element is rarely mentioned.[24] Indeed, the only major original Carolingian work in this genre to survive is a poem dated to 848 on the twelve months by Wandalbert, a monk of Prüm in the Rhineland, describing, in order, for each its: name, zodiac sign, appropriate rural activities (*culturis*) and meteorological characteristics.[25]

Wandalbert's poem on the monthly cycle is clearly within the literary Classical tradition, drawing heavily on Virgil and Ovid for its imagery. References to Christian religious festivals are totally absent. The poem is notable for its detailed interest in field sports: fowling, fishing, and particularly hunting of large game such as stags in September which Wandalbert notes was a particular passion of the Franks.[26] The often-detailed agricultural activities, of which there are several for each month, appear to be based on first-hand knowledge and observation, and the "labors" have been adapted "to the cooler and wetter seasonal climates of north-western Europe" (see Table 1).[27] Nevertheless, the work is clearly a literary amusement, written "at the urging of a friend", and is transmitted in only one ninth-century manuscript.[28]

Still, the model of a "practical" calendar of principal agricultural labors appropriate to each month would have been known to Charlemagne's intellectuals. Significantly, it was only Palladius, the most "monthly" of the Roman writers, who experienced something

---

[23]) In addition to Butzer, "Classical Tradition", see: Fussell, *Classical Tradition*, esp.Chap.2; and particularly, Gaulin, "Tradition et pratiques".

[24]) *Capitulare de Villis*, MGH, pp.84-5; there is an excellent facsimile edition and transcription of Cod.Guelf 254 Helmst. from the Herzog August Library, Wolfenbüttel, with modern commentary by Brühl, *Capitulare de Villis*, esp.pp.7-8 (Introduction), 57 (c.15) and 58 (c.25).

[25]) Wandalbert, *Carmina*, pp.567-8, 604-16 (see below, "Appendix", for the Latin text from

Dümmler's MGH edition and my parallel English translation of this work); *cf.* the comments on this as a source for agricultural history in Kuchenbuch, *Bäuerliche Gesellschaft*, esp.pp.36-7, 102,107; and Butzer, "Classical Tradition", pp.562-4.

[26]) "Venandi Francos docuit studiosa voluptas", Wandalbert, *Carmina*, p.613.

[27]) Butzer, "Classical Tradition", p.578, with his Table 1 on p.587 for a monthly synopsis of activities which differs somewhat from mine.

[28]) "hortatu compulsus amici", Wandalbert, *Carmina*, pp.616, 568.

of a vogue in the early ninth century.[29] Altogether six ninth-century manuscripts of the thirteen books (Introduction + one book for each of the 12 months) survive, the earliest from St Denis and dated to the first third of the century. Three other ninth-century manuscripts are, like it, also from northeast France, and one each comes from the Loire Valley and from the Netherlands or western Germany. The latest editor traces the manuscript tradition back to an archetype from northeast France, an area which, as we shall see, is also important for the transmission of the iconographic elements of the labors of the months.[30]

Finally, in the visual arts there are the predominately seasonal friezes, murals and, particularly, mosaics, dating primarily from the 2nd-4th centuries, which appear to have been especially popular in North Africa.[31] The early-3rd century mosaic from El Djem, Tunisia, is remarkable for its grid-like calendrical arrrangement of the months (Plate 3), and the two late-4th/early-5th century circular calendar mosaics from Carthage echo the iconography of the Codex-Calendar of 354. Such mosaics often include vivid and realistic vignettes of rural life into their generally seasonal arrangements. The El Djem mosaic, although composed primarily of references to the ritual year, also incorporates seasonal agricultural pictures for July and September. The, unfortunately, now incomplete seasonal mosaic (2nd/3rd cent.) discovered in southeastern France at St Romain-en-Gal and now in the Louvre contains the most vivid and engaging of these genre pictures which are organized completely around the cycle of the Four Seasons, not the succession of the months.[32]

All in all there was an abundance of visual, literary and practical source-material available to Carolingian intellectuals and artists for a reinvention of the Classical calendrical tradition. Indeed, it was almost too rich, for these sources suggested a wide variety of potential events and rural activities for each of the months whereas the Classical tradition, exemplified for us in the *Libri Carolini*'s derisive characterization and in Filocalus' calendar, personified the month by a single person, with a single set of seasonal attributes. This brings us back to Charlemagne.

C. Charlemagne's Months

Anyone familiar with Einhard's *Life of Charlemagne* will have noted the *Libri Carolini*'s references to the twelve winds and the twelve months, since Charlemagne tried, unsuccessfully, to "Frankify" their names. Einhard's "biography" provides us with many details and insights seldom available for early-medieval rulers. But, far from being narrowly biographical in a personal sense, Einhard's purpose in the Chapter 29 of his *Vita* clearly

---

[29]) Gaulin, "Tradition et pratiques", p.113.

[30]) Rodgers, *Introduction to Palladius*, pp.66-7.

[31]) Overview in Stern,"Les calendriers romains", Table I, between pp.468-9; Parrish, *Season Mosaics*, pp.52, 113-20, 156-60; Slim, "Eternal Time".

[32]) See the vignettes of seasonal agricultural activities from the St Romain-en-Gal mosaic in Stern, "Les calendriers", Pl.XIX, nrs 49-53.

incorporated an imperial political program.³³ The Chapter begins by stating that, "After assuming the dignity of the Imperial Title (*nomen*)", on Christmas Day in 800, Charlemagne set about reforming the law-codes of his own Frankish people and those "of all the other peoples who were under his authority". Likewise, he caused to be written down and committed to memory, "Those most ancient and barbaric songs by which the deeds and the battles of previous kings were celebrated", and he undertook a grammar of the Frankish language. Finally, he renamed the Twelve Months according to "his own language" (*iuxta propriam linguam*), since up to then the Franks (somewhat surprisingly) had used a mixture of Latin and "barbarian", vernacular names (= pagan: *partim Latinis, partim barbaris nominibus*). With regard to the Winds, he not only gave them Frankish names, but also increased the number to twelve, since previously scarcely more than the names of the four [cardinal] winds had been known (*cum prius non amplius quam vix quattuor ventorum vocabula possent inveniri*).

These activities were not just expressions of Charlemagne's personal interests. Rather, they were intended as assertions of claims to imperial legitimacy and authority: as lawgiver, as guardian and renewer of Frankish national traditions, and as unifier of a diverse empire. It is within this imperial political context that the naming of the Months and the Winds, which follow directly in this remarkable passage, must be seen.³⁴ Indeed, Charlemagne here was squarely within the Roman tradition, since the Roman Emperors as guarantors of natural order and harmony had, "use[d] the Seasons as visual symbols of the imperial dominion, imperial happiness [*felicitas*, that is, good fortune, success, luck], and imperial grace".³⁵ And, of course, the association of the Winds with the Seasons was both ancient and intimate.³⁶

This Classical model was not without Carolingian echoes. The Roman imperial motto of "felicitas temporum" and its variants was incorporated, in a somewhat denatured form, into the final section of the well-known Carolingian ruler acclamations, the *laudes regiae* where the King, perhaps, is less the guarantor than the recipient of prosperity: "Feliciter! Tempora bona habeas."³⁷ In the

---

³³) Einhard, *Vita Karoli Magni*, pp.33-4; there is a convenient edition of the text with facing German translation in Rau, *Quellen*, pp.200/1.

³⁴) The notion of "unification" or "uniformity" (*Vereinheitlichung*) is emphasized by Geuenich, "Volkssprachige Überlieferung", pp.124-5; on this point cf.also the more general remarks by Elias, *Time*, pp.53-6.

³⁵) Hanfmann, *Season Sarcophagus*, p.184; followed by MacCormack, *Art and Ceremony*, pp.112-3, 127, 172, 218-9.

³⁶) Hanfmann, *Season Sarcophagus*, pp.121-22, 252-3; Raff, "Ikonographie", esp.p.85-6 for discussion of a mural of the female Seasons and the male Winds from the "Domus Aurea Neronis" in Rome (18th-century copy in Raff, Abb.18, p.85), and p.89 for an altar relief from a Mithraeum in *Carnuntum*.

³⁷) Hanfmann, *Season Sarcophagus*, pp.166-73; Kantorowicz, *Laudes Regiae*, pp.14-20. For this and the following, see also the comments Folz, *Coronation of Charlemagne*, pp.80-3, 231-3. There is an interesting set of royal *laudes*,

related apotheosis of the Franks as a royal people in the longer "Prologue" to the *Lex Salica*, composed in the royal chancery in the 760s, Christ is to grant "felicitatem tempora".[38] Early-medieval rulers, including Charlemagne's grandson, Charles the Bald (though not Charlemagne himself) adopted an iconography in their portraits which is based compositionally on the Sun God surrounded by the Four Seasons or *Horae*, where, as a concession to Christian tradition, the Seasons have been replaced by personifications of the (four) Cardinal Virtues.[39]

But, in contrast, Charlemagne's new names for the months were both highly original (or idiosyncratic) and were completely divorced from the Classical tradition as were the less-colorful names for the twelve winds.[40] Possibly this signals an accommodation to Theodulf's views in the *Libri Carolini* where he notes contemptuously that the Classical, "gentile" names of the week-days and the months in use are derived, "for the most part from pagan falsehoods".[41] Rather, agricultural/rural activities dominate the new names for the months, accounting for six successive months from May through October, the most active portion of the agricultural year. The major agricultural regimes, arable, pastoral and (possibly) silviculture, though, surprisingly, not horticulture are included:[42]

---

probably commissioned by Bishop Baturich of Regensburg for the coronation of Ludwig the German in 826 which also includes at the end the threefold acclamation, "Feliciter. Tempora bona habeant", i.e. the Emperor Louis, King Ludwig and Bishop Baturich (Munich, Bayerische Staatsbibliothek, Clm 14510, fos.40ʳ-41ʳ; MS described in Andrieu, *Les 'Ordines Romani'*, pp.233, 107-8; Kantorowicz, p.106). See also below for Baturich.

[38]) D texts: *Lex Salica*, p.6; the emended E texts read: "felicitatem atque sanitatem per infinita secula", ibid.,p.7; Kantorowicz, *Laudes Regiae*, pp.58-9.

[39]) See Hanfmann, *Season Sarcophagus*, vol.1, p.184, and, vol.2, Plate 82 (Cat.Nr 18), for an 18th-century copy of the representation of the Sun God with the four *Horae* of the Seasons from the wall paintings in the "Domus Aurea Neronis", Rome; Schramm, *Deutsche Kaiser*, Plate 41, p.313, for a representation of Charles the Bald with the Four Virtues from the Bible of S.Paolo fuori le Mura, with Commentary to Plates 40 and 41, pp.54-6, 170-2. The representation of the Sun God from a now-lost mural in the "Domus Aurea Neronis" should be viewed within the context of the Seasons and the Winds cited above (Raff, "Ikonographie", pp.85-6). There is an extended discussion of Charles' representation in the Bible at S.Paolo fuori le mura in Staubach, *Rex Christianus*, pp.221-3, 234-61. Staubach does not consider explicitly the transformed seasonal elements (*horae*), but he does discuss the Virtues in comparable terms as binding heaven and earth, and he explores the connections of the dedicatory poem to the fertility of the consort (pp.255-9).

[40]) Schramm, "Bedeutung von Zahl und Winkel"; Betz, "Karl der Große und die lingua theodisca", pp.304-5.

[41]) "...nomina dierum et mensium gentilium vanitatibus plerumque nominantur", (*Libri Carolini*, p.16). *Cf.* Nees, *Tainted Mantle*, p.118.

[42]) *Cf.Capitulare de Villis*, c.70 (MGH, pp.90-1; Brühl, p.62) and below.

I. Seasonal Texts and Images

May: Pasture (*Winne-*)Month, probably when livestock first were allowed back into the pastures after the grass had recovered from winter. This name may have a military connotation because in 756 the annual muster of the Frankish army had been shifted from March to May to allow the newly-formed mounted squadrons (*scarae*) adequately to prepare their horses.[43]

June: Fallow (*Brach-*)Month, when the fallow (unplanted) fields in the arable rotation system of Northern Europe were plowed up to aerate and to dry them.[44] Plowing up the fallow is often interpreted to document an innovation of the period, the three-field rotation system.[45] But the major Roman agricultural writers all include plowing at this time, particularly to break up (*proscindere*) cold lands for cultivation.[46]

July: Hay (*Hewi-*)Month, when the grass growing in the meadows first was mowed.

August: Harvest (*Aran-*)Month, when the principal grain harvest took place.

September: Wood (*Witu-*)Month, possibly a time for cutting building-timber or, alternatively, when pigs first were driven into the woods to fatten them on the mast of acorns and beechnuts (pannage). In a rare calendrical reference, the "Capitulare de Villis" notes that the royal estate-managers, the bailiffs or "iudices", were to determine the extent of the annual pannage at the beginning of September.[47]

October: Vintage (*Windume-*)Month, when the grapes were gathered for winemaking.

Three of the months' names are neutrally seasonal but not totally convincing:

January: Winter (*Wintar-*)Month, which is mid-winter but does not correspond either to the traditional Classical beginning of Winter on 10 November and its end on 7 February, or to the Winter Solstice on 21/22 December.

March: Spring (*Lentzin-*)Month, which does mark the Vernal Equinox on or about 21 March but is very early for the onset of Springtime in Northern Europe which is usually associated with April (e.g. France) or even May (e.g. Germany; see below for the discussion of the May illustration of the

---

[43]) Fried, *Weg in die Geschichte*, pp.241-2; Ganshof, *Frankish Institutions*, pp.62, 155. Wandalbert of Prüm seems to play upon this in his calendrical poem for May (*Carmina*, pp.608-9).

[44]) Lynn White conflates the month-name with its pictorial depiction by referring to June consistently as "Ploughing Month" (*Medieval Technology*, pp.56, 70).

[45]) White, *Medieval Technology*, pp.69-70. Wilhelm Abel provides a useful schemmatic of the three-field crop rotation system in his "Landwirtschaft 500-900", pp.95-96 (see below, Figure).

[46]) Varro I,32 (pp.256/7); Columella XI,ii,46 (pp.96/7); Palladius VII,3 (p.162).

[47]) "De pastione autem Kal.Septemb. indicare faciant, si fuerit an non" (c.25, MGH, p.85; Brühl, p.58).

Salzburg pictures). However, it is designated as the first month of that season by the late-fourth-century Mosel poet, Ausonius.[48]

November: Autumn (*Herbist*-)Month, at the very beginning of which on 9 November, as we just saw, the Classical autumn <u>ended</u>.

Since there is only one month's separation in each seasonal succession (January-March; November-January), the implied seasons are strangely short and the identification of the "missing" "Summer-Month" is not obvious.

Two months' names, April and December, appear to have specifically Christian connotations deriving from the major festivals of Easter and Christmas. This does not surprise. During the early Carolingian period, efforts to regularize the observance of church festivals and holydays were intense.[49] Moreover, following the anointing of Pippin the Short as King in 751, the "Frankish Royal Annals" begin to note with some regularity the extraordinary solemnities which marked these festivals at the royal Court. Apparently, the public prominence which the Carolingian rulers directed towards Easter and Christmas derived in part from their concept of their now divinely-established authority, so that the festivals themselves became an, "exercise of lordship, indeed, beyond that a continuous renewal of the covenant between the King and God".[50]

April: Easter (*Ostar*-)Month, which Feast could also fall in March.[51] Perhaps, this month-name is a direct borrowing from the Anglo-Saxon names for the months discussed by Bede in his "De Temporum Ratione" of 725.[52] April or "Eosturmonath" is the only possible Christian name amongst the ten, but Bede gives it, too, a heathen derivation: "formerly it took its name from a goddess of theirs who was called Eostre and for whom they celebrated festivals at that time".[53] In view of the profound influence of Anglo-Saxon scholars, especially Alcuin, on the Frankish Court and Church, some trace of this well-known and widely-copied work would not be unusual.

December: Holy (*Heilag*-)Month, obviously a reference to Christmas, the New Year's day of the Frankish calendar. The old Anglo-Saxon "Halegmonath" was, interestingly, September, the pagan "mensis sacrorum".

One last month:

---

[48]) *Ecloga* VII, 18 (pp.192/3).

[49]) Finck von Finckenstein, "Fest- und Feiertage".

[50]) "...eine Ausübung der Herrschaft, ja darüber hinaus eine stetige Erneuerung des Bündnisses zwischen dem König und Gott", Fleckenstein, *Hofkapelle*, p.37, see pp.40-41 for the corresponding calendar of itineraries.

[51]) There are ten possible days in March (22nd-31st), *vs.* 25 in April (1st-25th).

[52]) Bede, *De Temporum Ratione Liber*, pp.329-32.

[53]) "...quondam a dea illorum quae Eostre vocabatur et cui in illo festa celebrabant nomen habuit": *Ibid.*, p.331.

I. Seasonal Texts and Images

February, uniquely carries the name "Hornung" without the suffix "*manoth*/month". The accepted etymology is somewhat contrived. In Old Norse the cognate word, *hornungr*, has a connotation of "bastard" which has been linked to the shortness of February in the Julian calendar.[54] Oddly, this is the only month name which survived in the vernacular, indicating, as does the lack of the suffix "month", that Charlemagne did not coin this name but, rather, appropriated it from contemporary popular usage.

Altogether Charlemagne's designations for the months incorporate the practical, secular preoccupations of a Northwest European agrarian society.[55] If this seems obvious, it is worth noting that, in contrast, the old Anglo-Saxon names for the months have only two agricultural references, the somewhat puzzling May/"Thrice Milked" (*Thrimilchi*) and the more prosaic August/"Grass-Month" (*Weodmonath*). But, it is perhaps, an oversimplification to describe these distinctive artifacts of human culture, as "more natural names" than their Roman counterparts.[56] Their content and structure is more complex than this, and their intent was evidently prescriptive as well as descriptive. Rather, there is clearly an attempt here to use reform of the calendar to embed, "the individual...in a world in which there are many other people, a social world, and many other natural processes..."[57]

Charlemagne's month-names, like the views of the *Libri Carolini*, were highly idiosyncratic and had an apparently short life. A complete rejection of the established usage derived from the Classical tradition was obviously too radical for contemporary acceptance.[58] This failure is unremarkable. Even in comparatively modern times the combination of a potent popular ideology and the coercive powers of the the state were insufficient to secure the lasting establishment of the new and supposedly "natural" nomenclature for the months devised during the French Revolution.[59] Nevertheless, Charlemagne's names for the months are

---

[54]) Perhaps, "outcast" in the sense of "exception" is more to the point here; see *Icelandic-English Dictionary*, ed.Cleasby-Vigfusson-Craigie, *sub verbo*.

[55]) Bullough, *Age of Charlemagne*, p.192; White, *Medieval Technology*: "Charlemagne's renaming of the months indicates how large the new agricultural cycle loomed in this thinking.", p.78.

[56]) "naturnahe", Borst,"Computus",p.21; *idem*, *Ordering of Time*, p.44.

[57]) Elias, *Time*, p.28.

[58]) It should be noted here that Charlemagne's bestowing exclusively *Frankish* names on the previously-macaronic Months and on the Winds violated his apparent "linguistic policy" which, while advancing the German vernacular, took full account of the needs of the large "Romania" within his Empire. This incongruity would account for the failure of the names to take hold generally if that had been Charlemagne's intent (Richter, "Sprachpolitik", pp.412-37, who cites the relevant passage from Einhard [p.416] but neglects to discuss it).

[59]) See the interesting discussion by Baczko, "Le Calendrier Républicain".

essential for understanding the (in contrast) very successful medieval iconographic tradition of the months. Unlike the Roman calendar's names for the months, Charlemagne's month-names focus predominately on a single characteristic seasonal event or agricultural activity (a "labor") for each month, in order to integrate human activity into an appropriate natural and supernatural order.

D. The Labors of the Months

The two early-ninth-century illustrations of the "Labors of the Months" produced in the area of Salzburg (Plate 4), lack any obvious artistic antecedents, and, accordingly, the manuscript context of these pictures is particularly crucial for their interpretation. The Salzburg manuscript (Codex 387; Plate 1) is the most important example of the successor hand to the "Alt-Salzburger" Stil II.[60] The second manuscript (Clm 210) is of uncertain origin although its hand shows influences from the important *scriptorium* at the monastery of Mondsee near Salzburg.[61] Their precise dating is a problem. Both contain references on their fos.7r to an "annus praesens" of 809/10 which, subsequently, has been altered to 818 (Clm 210) and 830 (Codex 387), respectively.[62] The pages containing the month-pictures are virtually identical (Clm 210, fo.91v; Codex 387, fo.90v), and Bischoff considered that the picture in Clm 210 was "traced" from that in Codex 387 which would imply the priority of Codex 387.[63] Any further consideration of their dating must take account of the circumstances of their production, a topic which is currently in the process of significant revision.[64]

---

[60]) For palaeographical analysis of both manuscripts see: Bischoff, *Schreibschulen*, Pt.II, pp.11-13, 34 (Munich, Clm 210); pp.60-1, 96-7 (Vienna, Codex 387).

[61]) Bischoff: the hands of Clm 210, "stehen zweifellos dem vornehmlich aus Mondsee belegten Stil nahe" (*Schreibenschulen* II, p.34).

[62]) Discussion of the dating in Bischoff, *Schreibschulen* II, pp.34, 96; and Rück, *Auszüge*, pp.12-13. The regnal years for Charlemagne, for example, have not been altered: "domnus carlus solus regnum suscepit, et deo protegente gubernat usque in presentem annum feliciter, qui est *annus regni eius XLII, imperii autem VIII* (i.e. 809)".

[63]) "...an dem Blatt mit den Monatsbildern läßt feststellen, daß durchgepaust wurde" (*Schreibschulen* II, p.34). On the basis of their respective appearances this conclusion is certainly plausible, but I was unable to confirm any physical tracing in my examination of the manuscripts although Bischoff does not seem to have been using the term metaphorically. See also the discussion of the "stimulus" below under "June". It is possible that both Salzburg manuscripts were copied from a now-lost exemplar. A.Borst has advanced evidence for a copy of this *computus* edition at the Aachen Court Library (*Buch der Naturgeschichte*, p.174, n.22), but it is not clear to me how the sequence of transmission was established. For the balance of this essay, I will continue to use the generally-accepted working hypothesis that Clm 210 is a contemporary copy of Codex 387 and that both were completed by or shortly before 818.

[64]) The following account in general follows Borst's, *Buch der Naturgeschichte*; the most relevant sections are pp.121-176, esp.Chap.V/1, pp.166-76. There is a somewhat condensed

I. Seasonal Texts and Images

Astronomy was an important subject of the "Carolingian Renaissance", and Charlemagne's personal interest in astronomical and computistical matters is well-known.[65] Einhard notes that this was Charlemagne's primary intellectual interest to which he gave "much time and labor". He learned the art of the computing dates (*artem conputandi*) and devoted himself to studying the course of the stars.[66] He corresponded with Alcuin regarding the calendar and astronomy, and presented him with a precious heavenly map of which he owned examples himself.[67] In the great capitulary, the "Admonitio Generalis" of 789, Charlemagne even had attempted to enforce knowledge of the *computus* as part of the standard clerical curriculum.[68]

Charlemagne's intense involvement with astronomical and calendrical matters was not prompted by intellectual curiosity. Rather, as Arno Borst argues, he was concerned here as elsewhere to fulfill the role of an authentic ruler by establishing harmony between Heaven and Earth and securing Divine Favor for his subjects and for himself. This required the correct celebration of the Church's feasts on the correct days, and to do this, the correct tools were necessary. Moreover, there was the overriding need to establish order and unity within the Empire. The months' names were one manifestation of this concern, but the concern with the *computus* was both more far-reaching and more complex in its political implications. Indeed, the whole medieval computistical tradition was less a search for a better "technology" (a problem essentially solved by Bede in the eighth century), than an elaborate metaphor about society, a "poetry about order".[69]

Beginning in 809 an expert Imperial Commission was set to work, perhaps under Charlemagne's cousin, Adalhard, Abbot of Corbie, to produce a definitive *computus* for use in the Empire.[70] The two Salzburg manuscripts have been considered an early

---

version of this argument in his, "Alkuin und die Enzykopädie von 809". Borst is editing these and related *computus* materials for the Monumenta Germaniae Historica.

[65]) McCluskey, "Astronomies ", pp.152*ff*.

[66]) Einhard, *Vita Karoli Magni*, c.25, (MGH, p.30; Rau, *Quellen*, pp.196/7). This section of Einhard has no parallel in his model, Suetonius.

[67]) Lohrmann, "Alcuins Korrespondenz", pp.96-7.

[68]) *Admonitio Generalis*, cap.72, pp.59-60. However, my examination of clerical inventories in Carolingian Bavaria revealed only one example of a *computus* (and epacts), in the possession of the obviously important minster at Thannkirchen in 855 ("Country Churches ", pp.11, 15-6). There is a recent, detailed content exegesis of the computistical works of Bede and Hrabanus Maurus, without any historical context, in: Englisch, *Artes Liberales*, pp.280-469.

[69]) Wallis, "Images of Order", p.47.

[70]) Borst, *Buch der Naturgeschichte*, pp.154-5. For the 809 redaction see also the, "Capitula, De quibus convocati compotiste interrogati fuerint...", MGH, Epistolae, vol.4, pp.565-7 (English translation in Jones, "Early Medieval Licensing Examination", pp.26-9); Bischoff, "Libraries and Schools", p.108.

result of this effort, the so-called "Three Book" edition, probably copied between 809 and 818 from a Court exemplar.[71] However, it now appears more likely that the version produced during Charlemagne's lifetime was the so-called "Seven Book" edition, and the two manuscripts from Bavaria, represent, rather, a later and isolated effort, completed in 818 under the direction of Archbishop Arn of Salzburg, to establish a different computistical direction.[72] For whatever reason, this effort was unsuccessful, and these two Bavarian *computus* manuscripts remained an isolated, intellectual dead-end.

As the title assigned to them, The Three-Book Computus, implies, these two Salzburg manuscripts are divided into three rather large and unwieldy sections or "Books".[73] The first section (99 caps.) contains the bulk of the computistical material but also includes a short but highly interesting martyrology (*Martyrologium excarpsatum*), an extended set of annual Easter tables running through the year 1063 (*i.e.* the end of Bedan cycle) with marginal historical notes, and extended excerpts from Bede's *De Temporum Ratione*.[74] The second section (11 caps.), contains a mixture of astronomical /astrological, meteorological and metrological excerpts from Classical authors including Pliny. The final, third section (51 caps.) contains Bede's *De Natura Rerum*, followed by another set of extensive tables on the lunar cycle.[75]

Each section or "Book" of these manuscripts contains one full-page illustration in addition to a number of smaller illustrations and diagramms in Book Two. In the Munich manuscript, Clm 210, at the very beginning of the second Book on folio 113v, opposite a page entitled "Excerptum de Astrologia" (fo.114r; "Hyginus philosophus"), is a full-page colored Planisphere with a Zodiac Circle superimposed on it. This illustration now is absent from the Vienna manuscript Codex 387 and evidently was lost along with with eleven additional, smaller illustrations of zodiac figures and constellations.[76]

---

[71]) For a discussion of this "Three Book" edition see: McGurk, "Carolingian Astrological Manuscripts", pp.317, 320-1; Eastwood, "Astronomies", pp.163-6; and the 1993 exhibition catalogue: *Karl der Grosse und die Wissenschaft*, p.38.

[72]) Their, apparently, substantial divergence from the other *computus* editions is discussed by Borst in *Buch der Naturgeschichte*, esp.pp.171-2.

[73]) There are detailed descriptions of Clm 210 and Codex 387 in: Rück, *Naturgeschichte*, pp.5-13; and of Codex 387 only in: Saxl, *Verzeichnis*, pp.79-81.

[74]) The martyrology is edited with commentary by McCulloh, "Martyrologium Excarpsatum". Some of the marginal notes from Clm 210 were published by G.Waitz under the title, "Annales S. Emmerammi Minores", reflecting the manuscript's sojurn there.

[75]) Bede, *De Natura Rerum Liber*.

[76]) Rück, *Naturgeschichte*, p.10; Saxl, *Verzeichnis*, p.80. The illustrations from Clm 210 are discussed in von Euw, "Künstlerische Gestaltung", *passim*. Two of the Plinian diagrams in this second section are wrong. For an analysis of these incorrect diagrams see: Eastwood, "Astronomies", p.166; and *idem*, "Plinian astronomical diagrams", pp.148-54. For a discussion of the Planisphere and other

I. Seasonal Texts and Images

In the third section or Book there is another full-page illustration of particular interest for our topic: a unique depiction of the Twelve Winds which stands opposite the chapter from Bede's *De Natura Rerum* on the "Ordo Ventorum" (Plate 5).[77] Both Einhard and Bede use the Classical figure of a circular "Wind Rose" to describe the Winds. Einhard lists Charlemagne's Frankish names for the twelve winds and their Classical counterparts in clockwise sequence beginning in the East; Bede begins in the North and lists the four cardinal winds in clockwise sequence along with the two Winds subordinate to each on its "right" and "left".[78] However, the illustration of the winds in these Salzburg manuscripts does not use the convention of the "Wind Rose". Rather, it attempts to compose the twelve winds in the form of a "Maiestas-Domini" picture where Christ is at the center and the four Evangelists and four principal Prophets are arrayed symmetrically around him![79] The resulting picture is absurd. Two of the subsidiary Winds, Aquilo (NE) and Vulturnus (EN) are at the center of the composition, and the peripheral sequence of the Cardinal Winds is disturbed by the intrusion of Austroafricus (SW) and Africus (WS) between Auster (S) and Zephyrus (W).[80] It is not difficult to grasp why this bizarre, albeit original approach to the Winds was without successors.

If the Twelve Winds were an iconographic fiasco, the Twelve "Labors of the Months", in contrast, were (ultimately) a surprising success. These somewhat crude but, nevertheless, lively and attractive pictures comprise the full-page illustration for the first section or "Book" of the Salzburg manuscripts where they are composed in a vertically-arranged set of three cartoon-like panels, each containing individual representations of four months. But unlike the other full-page pictures of the Planisphere/Zodiac in the second "Book" or the Winds in the third, which are blank on the backsides of their folios, this ensemble of the months is completely integrated into the surrounding text. The pictures are included in the computistical discussion from Bede's *De*

---

astronomical devices depicted see: Stevens, "*Compostistica et astronomica*", pp.47-9.

[77]) Clm 210, fo.139r; Codex 387, fol.140r (the sequence of 8-folio gatherings is disturbed in this section of Codex 387, fos.137r-146v; Rück, *Naturgeschichte*, p.11).

[78]) Bede, *De Natura Rerum Liber*, p.218.

[79]) Raff, "Ikonographie", pp.145-6; von Euw, "Künstlerische Gestaltung", p.259. For this genre see: Van Der Meer, *Maiestas Domini*, pp.328-37, where such a picture in the Bible of Charles the Bald at S.Paulo fuori le Mura is discussed (Fig.77, p.335; see above for a discussion of the royal portrait in this Bible). For some reason this illustration of the Winds is not discussed in the recent and otherwise exhaustive study by Obrist

although she does refer to diagrams in these two manuscripts: "Wind Diagrams", p.63; *cf.*pp.66-75 ("Personifications of Winds").

[80]) The representations of the Winds are in the form of male busts, modeled after Roman portraits, where the artist has unknowingly copied a female head for a male in depicting Austroafricus; the only iconographical detail identifying the Winds as such are the facing poses of Septentrio (N) and Subsolanus (E) vigorously puffing at each other (Raff, "Ikonographie", p.146).

Temporum Ratione, and their precise location is significant, since they are placed on a *verso* page where they face, on the opposite *recto* page, the beginning of Book I's Cap.73, "De Signis XII Mensium", which discusses the zodiac signs and designations associated with the months.[81] Here we would normally expect an illustration of the zodiac on the facing page, but, as we just have noted, that picture is reserved for the second Book. Moreover, in the sequence of Bede's work, these pictures of the months replace Chapter XV, "De Mensibus Anglorum" where the Old English vernacular names for the months are discussed.[82]

Considerable care obviously has been taken in both manuscripts to ensure a visually-pleasing compositional ensemble for these facing pages in the form of a diptych. The Chapter from Bede includes Ausonius' *Eclogue* on the zodiac names for the months which is transcribed in short lines in both manuscripts.[83] The rest of the text in Clm 210 on the same page as the poem (92r) separates the Chapter title and alternates long and short lines in contrast to the run-on format of the preceding and following pages. The scribe of Codex 387 departs from the strict 25 line page format on the preceding recto page (90r) to insert the last two words of Cap.72 (= Bede, Chapter XIV, "De Mensibus Graecorum": "esse moratur") on to an exceptional 26th line. This ensured the first line at the top of the following text page (91r) would be occupied by the relevant title line for the chapter on the "Signs of the Twelve Months". Similarly, the scribe of Clm 210 saved a line on his facing page (92r) by inserting the last word of the preface to Ausonius' Eclogue, "heroicis", on to the end of the preceding short line. This allowed him to include the last words of the paragraph following the poem (*contingentium obsident*) with space to spare on the page facing the pictures.

This last point may provide another clue for understanding the pictures, since this paragraph from Bede concludes a short discussion noting the non-congruence between the zodiac signs and the calendar months.[84] Thus, a zodiac sign which included

---

[81]) Clm 210, 91v, Codex 387, 90v. The text is excerpted from Bede's Chapter XVI (*De Temporum Ratione Liber*, pp.332-7).

[82]) This Chapter has been omitted from both Salzburg manuscripts. It was known, however, in Carolingian Bavaria (Munich, Bavarian State Library, Clm 14725 [fos.63v-65r] from the library of St Emmeram, Regensburg but produced in NE France; Bischoff, *Schreibschulen*, Part I, p.253) See above for the possible influence of this section from Bede on Charlemagne's name for the month of April.

[83]) *Ecloga* VII, 16, pp.190/1, which begins the order of the months with January rather than April as in Bede (*De Temporum Ratione Liber*, p.333).

[84]) "Qui, quod de uno decembri specialiter dixit [i.e. Ausonius], de caeteris utique generaliter intelligendum signavit quia videlicet singula quaeque signorum medio suo mense terminentur, a medio priore sumant exortum. [...] Undeque gyrum caeli rotundissimum per lineam zodiaci circuli, quasi per zonam quandam amplissimae spere circumdatam distincti ordines gemmarum xii sese invicem contingentium obsident." (Clm 210, fo.92r; Jones, p.334). The only notable textual omission on this facing page is Bede's observation, "De quorum positione strictim

I. Seasonal Texts and Images

parts of two calendar months was not a fully-suitable representation of either. This problem, however, was solved by the new iconography of the "labors" advanced at this point in the Salzburg manuscripts, since each month possessed a special representation or activity unique to it! Thus, based upon both form and content, the manuscript placement of the Salzburg "labors" appears to be thoroughly conscious and highly programmatic in proposing a new iconography for the months in contrast to the old one of the zodiac.[85]

Georg Swarzenski was the first scholar to present and analyze these pictures in detail within his larger examination of early-medieval Salzburg painting.[86] He thought it, "most probable that they should be considered original innovations of the Carolingian period."[87] In general, Swarzenski's basic judgement has stuck, and these Salzburg pictures have been used frequently in modern historical works to interpret and to illustrate Carolingian rural scenes of, "peasants, fully clothed and hard at work with their tools, that is, the local work-a-day scene".[88]

Since then the art historians James Carson Webster, George Hanfmann, and Henri Stern, and, most recently, the historian, Georges Comet have added to the pioneering work of Riegl and established an analytical framework which distinguishes between a "Classical" and a "Medieval" calendrical tradition (Exhibit).[89] Indeed, this development was already underway in late Antiquity as evidenced by the Codex-Calendar of 354 which applied conventional iconographic personifications of the Classical Seasons to individual months. As we shall see, the Salzburg pictures also represent a transitional stage in this development, incorporating both "Classical" and "Medieval" elements.

Both Swarzenski and Stern have related these pictures to poetic cycles of the months.[90] However, the value of these somewhat later poems is as nearly contemporary gloss on the pictures and as a witness to wider interest in the subject matter, obviously not as a potential source. The more closely connected poems from the so-called

---

nescientes instruere obsecro scientibus oneri non sit", between the sentences indicated by [...].

[85]) Thus, Bridget Ann Henisch has the problem turned around at the beginning of her exemplary article when she states for the calendar illustrations: "The presence of the occupation scene is readily understood...The presence of the zodiac sign needs a little more explanation." ("In Due Season", p.309).

[86]) *Salzburger Malerei*, pp.12-21.

[87]) "...so ist es bei den Monatsbildern im höchsten Grade wahrscheinlich, daß sie als originale Erfindungen der karolingischen Zeit anzusehen sind" (*Salzburger Malerei*, p.15).

[88]) "...schwer arbeitende und vollständig bekleidete Bauern samt ihrem Werkzeug dar, mithin den örtlichen Alltag" (Borst, *Buch der Naturgeschichte*, p.173).

[89]) Webster, *Labors of the Months*; Hanfmann, *Season Sarcophagus*; Stern, "Poésies" and *"Les calendriers"*; Comet, "Les calendriers médiévaux".

[90]) *Salzburger Malerei*, pp.16-21; "Poésies", pp.142-9.

"Carmina Salisburgensia", dated to the late 850s, do suggest a possible visual source for the pictures of the "Labors", since another set of poems, "De ordine conprovincialium pontificum", within the same collection celebrates certain bishops from the Province of Salzburg.[91] These latter poems on the bishops clearly served as legends for a set of portrait murals in the Salzburg archiepiscopal palace.[92] And it is possible that the manuscript illuminations of the months were, themselves, originally conceived as murals or as mosaics. Salzburg, in the heart of the *villa* landscape of *Noricum Ripense*, had been a significant provincial center for both arts in Roman times, and a numerous and coherent Latin-speaking population, often of high social status, survived well into the early Middle Ages as preservers of Classical cultural tradition.[93]

Certainly, the pronounced four-panel division in which the pictures are displayed, each panel incorporating three months in sequence without internal division (see especially the unique combination of November and December), is consistent with an architectural arrangement, a suspicion reinforced by the similar arrangement of the El Djem calendrical mosaic (Plate 3).[94] However, it must be added that the four panels, the first of which begins with January, lack the explicit seasonal order (and emblems) of the El Djem mosaic and correspond neither to the late-Antique conception of the four Seasons as represented, for example, by Ausonius in his Eclogues, nor to Charlemagne's seasonal divisions.[95] Moreover, the pictures disregard the Bedan excerpt from Ausonius' Eclogue VII, 16 on the facing folio which begins the sequence of the months with April, not January. Thus, in the Salzburg pictures the Classical Four Seasons have been replaced completely by a strictly calendrical twelve-month sequence beginning in January.

---

[91] *Carmina Salisburgensia*, pp.644-6, Nrs X, XI; Bischoff, *Schreibschulen* II, pp.160-1.

[92] Swarzenski, *Salzburger Malerei*, pp.12-3.

[93] For general overviews see Alföldy, *Noricum*, esp.Map, p.130, and Czysz, *Römer in Bayern*, esp.pp.243-4; for Salzburg see Heger, *Salzburg in römischer Zeit*, pp.120-8, on mosaics and frescoes, and the relevant sections of *Geschichte Salzburgs*. For specialized studies of Roman mosaics see Kenner, "Römische Mosaiken", pp.86-8, and Jobst, *Römische Mosaiken*. There is a short review of early Christian frescoes in Pillinger, "Die malerische Innenausstattung". I have not found a single example of clearly seasonal art in any of this Roman material from Raetia II and Noricum Ripense. It does, however, document the high technical and artistic level of the Salzburg workshops down into at least the fourth century. The evidence for the "Roman" population of early-medieval Salzburg is discussed by Messner, "Salzburgs Romanen".

[94] Comet, "Les calendriers", citing Emile Mâle, notes the correspondence to the product of the Trinity (3) and the Elements (4), p.42, n.20; *cf*.Brunner, *Oppositionelle Gruppen*, pp.69-70. For an example of this mentality related to the Seasons, see Alcuin's letter of 798-802 to Arn (*Epistolae*, Nr 243, pp.389-90).

[95] *Ecloga* VII, 18, pp.192/3. *E.g*. Winter: December-February; the "classical" beginning of Winter was actually 10 November. The first panel contains both January, Charlemagne's "Winter-Month", and March, the "Spring-Month".

I. Seasonal Texts and Images

Like Charlemagne's names for the months, the subject matter of these twelve pictures is diverse and, occasionally, enigmatic. But, unlike the month nomenclature, which represents an attempted complete break with the Classical tradition, these pictures (whose exclusively male figures, we may note with relief, are all decently clad) reflect an intermediate station on the way from antique personifications to medieval labors. The explicitly "Classical" elements are concentrated in the first five months of the year. Three of the illustrations stand obviously within the Classical tradition. Like some of the illustrations in the Codex-Calendar of 354 which these particular months mirror, they apply a general seasonal motif to a specific month. In addition, they correspond directly to the iconography of the Four Seasons as recorded in the *Libri Carolini*, while a fourth, for October (see below), also represents an agricultural activity:

January: a man warming his hands by a fire. This is the second seasonal emblem for winter mentioned in the *Libri Carolini* as we might expect from the "Winter-Month". In the Codex-Calendar a man is making an offering into a burning brazier; Comet interprets the Salzburg illustration as a Christian "misreading" of this pagan scene.[96]

February: a man with a large bird held in or perched on his right hand and with two smaller ones tucked into his left arm. Clearly, this image depicts fowling and corresponds to the fourth seasonal emblem for winter cited in the *Libri Carolini* ("capturing birds enfeebled by excessive cold"). In the Codex-Calendar a woman holds a waterfowl.

May: a man bearing flowers, corresponding to the *Libri Carolini's* image of Spring "verdant with flowers" (see below for April). The Codex-Calendar also has a "flower-bearer" figure, a conventional Classical representation of Spring, for this month.[97]

The seven months beginning with June all represent agricultural scenes or "labors" and anticipate the fully-developed "Medieval" tradition. Except for the just noted anomoly of October (see below), there are no obvious correspondences to the Codex-Calendar:

June: a plowman directing a plow-team, apparently breaking up the fallow rather than preparing for immediate sowing: Charlemagne's "Fallow" month (see discussion above). This image clearly draws on a stock Classical source which must have been widely known in the Carolingian period. The Roman mosaic from St Romain-en-Gal and the nearly contemporary Carolingian Utrecht and Stuttgart Psalters, also depict a two-ox team directed by a plowman with a

---

[96] "Les calendriers", pp.43-4; see also below for April.

[97] See, for example, the discussion in Klibansky, *Saturn and Melancholy*, p.294.

"stimulus" and pulling an unwheeled "aratrum"/ard plow.[98]

July: a man carrying a scythe used to mow hay: Charlemagne's "Hay" month. The picture remains close to the Classical tradition of passive personification with attribute, since the man is not actively engaged as are the other "laborers" of this group. The comparable figures from the Utrecht Psalter and the somewhat later Martyrology of Wandalbert of Prüm are, in contrast, very active (see below). Stern has proposed the partially-surviving relief on the Roman arch at Reims (2nd/3rd cent.) as a possible source for this motif in July.[99]

August: a man with a sickle harvesting the main grain crop: Charlemagne's "Harvest" month.

September: a man sowing seed, that is the winter crop, which usually consisted of wheat and rye in northern Europe. In Wandalbert of Prüm's mid-ninth century poem on the months, spelt (a variety of wheat) is mentioned in September.[100]

October: a man simultaneously picking grapes and placing them into a vat: Charlemagne's "Vintage" month. But this is precisely the *conflated* emblem attributes assigned by the *Libri Carolini* to the season of Autumn rather than a realistic genre scene.[101] In addition, the composition of this picture clearly echoes the pose of the figure in the Codex-Calendar for September, a suitable time for the vintage in Italy (Plates 2 and 4).

November: a man spearing or prodding a pig, that is, either a hunting scene or, possibly, a swineherd driving his charge into the woods for fattening on the mast of fallen nuts, a common Autumn scene, which then issues in the connected

---

[98]) For the "stimulus" see White, *Farm Equipment*, pp.210-1. This picture for June contains the only significant difference of detail between Vienna Codex 387 and Munich Clm 210, since Codex 387 depicts the "stimulus" while Clm 210 seems to show a four-stranded lash. For the plow *cf*.Dufrenne, *Les illustrations*, pp.169-70, where, I believe, there is some unnecessary mystification. The Utrecht, Stuttgart and Salzburg plows are clearly "body-ards" (for the Utrecht and Stuttgart plows, respectively, see the representations in Dufrenne, *Les illustrations*, Plate 97, and the unpaginated frontispiece color plate to Cat.Nr 108A in *Un village*) . The St Romain-en-Gal plow may be a closely-related "sole-ard" (possibly the elusive "Roman" plow-type, to which Dufrenne alludes; see Stern, "Les calendriers", Plate XIX, nr 52), as is the plow in the 1023 Montecassino illustration, based upon a Carolingian original, to the section on the Seasons, apparently, here Winter, in Hrabanus Maurus' encyclopædia (*Miniature sacre e profane*, Plate LIII). There is a full discussion of these plow types in White, *Agricultural Implements*, pp.123-45, esp.126-8; see also below.

[99]) "Poésies", pp.149-50; "Les calendriers", Table I.

[100]) "Hinc quoque farra suis prodest committere sulcis", Wandalbert, *Carmina*, p.613 (see below, "Appendix").

[101]) Dufrenne, *Les illustrations*, p.89, n.132.

I. Seasonal Texts and Images

slaughter scene in December. At least, this is the interpretation of the second Salzburg month-poem.[102] This image may be an attempt to represent Charlemagne's "Autumn-Month" although, as we saw earlier, it also might be appropriate to September, the "Wood-Month". Stern also sees the Roman arch at Reims as a possible source for this double scene in November/December.[103]

December: a man with a long knife, ready to slaughter November's pig. This highly original, even unique, artistic combination of two monthly scenes implies that the pig had survived November! However, this solution would be more convincing if the pig were orientated in the opposite direction, *away from* November and *towards* December. Since slaughter was closely connected with year-end feasting, particularly at Christmas, and the salting and smoking of the pork is mentioned prominently by Wandalbert, this image is quite appropriate to the month.[104] However, we should note that the larger part of December is occupied by a penitential season of fasting: Advent!

The two remaining months are very enigmatic and require extended discussion:

March: a man holding a bird in his right hand and a writhing snake in his left. This strange combination is implied clearly by the gloss of the second Salzburg "Song": "March brings forth snakes, it rejoices in the [song of the ?] bird (*alite*), it heralds the mild seasons with its foliage".[105] The seasonal imagery, e.g. the emergence of snakes from their hibernation at the first warm weather, is certainly apt, albeit, like Charlemagne's name for March, somewhat premature for Northern Europe. Unfortunately, this image cannot be fitted easily into any well-established iconographic scheme.[106]

One, admittedly remote, possibility is to link this scene to the most remarkable of the surviving Roman mosaics in Austria, an explicitly Christian work from a cemetery church in Carinthia and dated to about the year 500. One of the scenes is an eagle attacking a serpent which is usually interpreted as a representation of Good triumphing over Evil, not totally inappropriate to a month in which Easter might fall. And, of course, "ales" does

---

[102] *Carmina Salisburgensia*, Nr XI: "Decidua porcos pascit quia glande Novimber" (p.646). Wandalbert mentions pannage in both October and November (*Carmina*, p.614; see below, "Appendix").

[103] "Poésies", pp.149-50; "Les calendriers", Table I.

[104] Wandalbert, *Carmina*, p.616 (see below, "Appendix").

[105] *Carmina Saliburgensia*, Nr XI, p.645; *cf.*Comet, "Les calendriers", p.80.

[106] I assume here that the serpent is a serpent and not a garbled representation of a reflex bow, in which case we have an equally difficult-to-place hunting scene; see the next month, April, for an analogous problem.

have the primary meaning of a bird of prey or eagle.[107]

But, there is, perhaps, a simpler, though more surprising, way to connect this illustration to Charlemagne's "Spring-Month". The important early-ninth-century Fulda monk and encyclopædist, Hrabanus Maurus, included the eagle and the snake as two (very unflattering) attributes of Jove/Jupiter in his discussion of the pagan gods (*modo in similitudinem aquilæ, propter quod puerum ad stuprum rapuerit, modo serpentem, quia reptaverit*).[108] These are precisely the attributes used in an important set of illustrations to Hrabanus' work copied in 1023 for a well-known Montecassino manuscript from a Carolingian model, which (it has been asserted) are "largely based on the ancient pictorial tradition" (Plate 6).[109] Jupiter is appropriate as a representation of Spring, since he, like Venus, was identified with the Sanguine humor which predominates in Springtime.[110] Possibly the Salzburg illustrator here again was copying a model, the implications of which, like January (see above), he did not understand or wished to ignore.

April: a man holding a sheaf in his right hand and pointing towards a tree in bud with his left hand; only the most far-fetched interpretation (the "arbor vitae") could connect this picture to Charlemagne's "Holy-Month"! The later Salzburg poet glosses this image as: "April bears bundles

---

[107]) Noll, *Frühes Christentum*, pp.95-9; Kenner, "Römische Mosaiken", pp.91-3, with unexplained doubts about the interpretation of the mosaic expressed by Henri Stern in the discussion on p.93. The name of a probable patron, Archbishop Arn of Salzburg, means "the Eagle" which, however, was translated as the Court pseudonym, "Aquila" (see below).

[108]) *De Universo Libri XXII*, Bk.XV, cap.vi (*De diis gentium*), col.429.

[109]) Klibansky, *Saturn and Melancholy*, pp.198, 309, Pl.12 (= *Miniature sacre e profane*, Plate CVIII); *cf.*Webster, *Labors*, p.40. It has been argued recently that these Montecassino illustrations cannot be based upon Antique sources because of the nudity prevalent in the depictions of the dieties, "very seldom rendered nude in antiquity" (Nees, *A Tainted Mantle*, pp.10-11, citing N.Himmelmann, *Antike Götter im Mittelalter*, Trierer Winckelmannsprogramme 7 [Mainz, 1986], pp.6-11, which I have not been able to consult). I find this conclusion surprising in view of the nude sculptures of male dieties which survive even from Roman Bavaria, Rhaetia and Noricum (*e.g.* for Mercury/Hermes, Apollo, and Mars in Czysz, *Römer in Bayern*, Abb.64, 66, and Alföldy, *Noricum*, Pls.36, 40-2). On the other hand, Hrabanus' description would leave open the possibility of a burlesque. Nor is such a conclusion incompatible with the poses of the relevant gods here [Plate 6] which, nevertheless are all modestly draped or otherwise appropriately covered. The Salzburg Jove/Jupiter, in contrast to the Montecassino figure, is fully dressed as are all the other figures in the Salzburg cycle. This may be only a recognition of the prudish sentiments noted in the *Libri Carolini* or may reflect a different model. While I think that the iconographic attribution proposed here is secure, the issue of a Classical model and the exact intent of the picture must remain open.

[110]) Klibansky, *Saturn and Melancholy*, pp.127-8, 187.

of green shoots as the earth blooms and the leaf buds on the tree".[111] Accordingly, this would be another seasonal personification in the Classical tradition like May, and we are left with a doublet of April-May (or even a triplet of March-April-May) declaring the vernal return of vegetation, analogous to November-December's pig but without its connecting "bridge" device.

The sheaf or bundle, however, has been a problem for modern commentators.[112] One possible solution is to assume that the illustrator has misread his (deteriorated?) model and substituted the sheaf for a Roman "cultellus" or pruning knife which was of the same shape and size, roughly like a modern machete.[113] Unfortunately, pruning is an activity appropriate to earlier months in the year and is usually depicted in connection with vines, not trees, with March being the preferred month. It is vaguely possible that this is an allusion to grafting which would make this picture the only one in the cycle connected to horticulture, a sphere of agricultural activity which is notably absent from Charlemagne's names for the months (see above). However, another (but closely related and more likely) alternative would be to see this picture as a depiction of the old practice known in Bavaria as "schnaiteln" where the first leaf-buds were cut for animal fodder to bridge the period in the Spring when hay supplies became scarce and the grass was not year ready for grazing.[114] This suggestion would explain the prominence of the buds on the tree and would anticipate well Charlemagne's "Pasture" month in May.

Despite these last two enigmatic pictures, agricultural and generally seasonal, not religious, elements predominate in the Salzburg cycle of illustrations as they do in Charlemagne's names for the months.

E. Comparisons and Perspectives

The only other possible Carolingian illustration of the labors of the months, albeit a very late one, is the set of illustrations contained in a manuscript of a calendrical martyrology also written in the mid-ninth century by Wandalbert of Prüm (Plate 7). The manuscript itself, now in the Vatican Library (MS Reg.lat.438), apparently dates to the late ninth century and probably was composed in the western part of Germany, possibly the Rhineland.[115] The pictures accompanying the Martyrology stand individually in the manuscript like the illustrations from the Codex-Calendar of 354, but unlike the ensemble panels of the Salzburg "Labors". They depict individual male figures, fully clothed except for June, and set within architectural frames, typically as passive

---

[111]) *Carmina Salisburgensia*, Nr XI, p.645; cf.Comet, "Les calendriers", p.80.

[112]) Swarzenski, *Salzburger Malerei*, p.18; Webster, *Labors*, pp.37, 129.

[113]) White, *Agricultural Implements*, pp.70-1.

[114]) I owe this interesting solution to Dr Gertrud Diepolder.

[115]) Riegl, "Mittelalterliche Kalendarillustration", pp.40-51; Webster, *Labors of the Months*, pp.41-6; Comet, "Les calendriers", pp.73-4.

personifications with seasonal (including zodiacal) attributes of the months. Only two of the eleven surviving months (September is missing), depict active agricultural "labors": a very vigorous figure mowing hay in July and harvester with sickle in August. The pictures in the Martyrology bear no relationship to Wandalbert's calendrical poem on the twelve months which is not included in this manuscript, and they have not been related to any other obvious literary source. Their appearance generally indicates, "that the miniaturist was following an antique cycle".[116]

For whatever reason, later German sources were less prolific in illustrations of the "labors of the months" than their French and Italian counterparts. Webster catalogues only five examples: two from the late-tenth century and three from the twelfth (Table 1).[117] Moreover, the diversity of themes for individual months, e.g. May, precludes any notion of a unified German "tradition", unlike twelfth-century France where a single image typically dominates each month. However, having said that, it is worth noting that the Salzburg sequence: June/Plowing, July/Mowing Hay, August/Reaping Grain, also predominates in this later German group and stands in contrast to the French cycles which never include plowing in June and which locate mowing and reaping back from July and August to the previous months, June and July, respectively.[118]

A final comparison of potential interest is to two early-ninth century psalters. The Utrecht Psalter was probably composed near Reims at the monastery of Hautvillers in the decade after the Salzburg pictures were completed.[119] Although its structure is not at all calendrical, it does contain numerous and vivid genre pictures of rural life, echoing the corresponding Psalms literally or metaphorically. Scenes of plowing, mowing, reaping, tending vines and the vintage are especially common. Cattle and sheep abound, though the domestic pig, which occupies so prominent a position in the "labors", is appropriately absent. The very dynamic forms of the compositions recall, in particular, the seasonal mosaic from St Romain-en-Gal.[120] We already have noted above that one specific archaeological detail links the Utrecht Psalter to the Salzburg "labors": the type of the plow of which, according to Dufrenne, "le calendrier illustré [from Salzburg]...en présente un exemple voisin".[121] With its undoubted "realism" of detail, the Utrecht Psalter is probably the best evidence for the complete stock of agricultural

---

[116]) Webster, *Labors of the Months*, p.43.

[117]) *Labors of the Months*, Nrs 28, 29, 87, 88, 89, respectively.

[118]) *Cf.*Stern, "Poesies", pp.145-50.

[119]) Dufrenne, *Les illustrations*, pp.89-93, 168-73, esp.Plate 97; Utrecht Psalter, complete facsimile edition with commentary in *Codices Selecti*.

[120]) Wormald, *Utrecht Psalter*, p.11, who also notes the inclusion of numerous personifications of the Psalmist's sun and moon, rivers and streams, an interesting response to the concerns of the *Libri Carolini*; Dufrenne, *Les illustrations*, p.89, n.132.

[121]) *Les illustrations*, pp.169-70.

I. Seasonal Texts and Images

genre-images available to our nearly-contemporary Salzburg artist.

The so-called Stuttgart Psalter is not so rich in agricultural material. It apparently was composed at St Germain-des-Prés in the first quarter of the ninth century and contains a very limited set of everyday scenes. However, three pictures, the tilling of vines, a plowing scene discussed above, and sowing, accompanying Psalms 79, 106, and 125, respectively, are relevant, and the last two parallel the months of June and September in the Salzburg pictures.[122]

F. Some Interim Art-Historical Conclusions

The Salzburg pictures conflate two Classical artistic traditions: the seasonal but non-calendrical genre-scene representation of agricultural activities as in the St. Romain-en-Gal mosaic, and the personification of the months as depicted in the Codex-Calendar of 354 or in the North African seasonal mosaics. To the extent that the Salzburg illustrations contain both passive personifications and pictures of active "labors", they represent a transition from the "Classical" to the "Medieval" calendrical model. Likewise, they are clearly "Medieval" in their exclusively monthly arrangement, single agricultural activity, and the absence of explicitly religious themes, but they are "Classical" in that they occur in a (largely) secular, not a sacred manuscript context. Nevertheless, I think that anyone familiar either with the earlier Codex-Calendar of 354 or with Wandalbert's later Martyrology will conclude that the demarcating line has been passed decisively in the direction of the Medieval model. Can we say more?

Charlemagne's names for the months, these Salzburg pictures and a number of other relevant seasonal works from Antiquity and the Middle Ages can be compared synoptically (Table 1). From this display and from the foregoing discussion we can attempt to identify the Classical and Caroline correspondences of the Salzburg pictures (Table 2). Altogether "Caroline" literary influences may account for as many as nine of the month pictures. The *Libri Carolini* contain emblems explicitly appropriated for the pictures of January, February, May and October, and these are precisely the months with the closest correspondence to the illustrations in the Codex-Calendar of 354! Charlemagne's activity-based names of the months correspond clearly to the depictions of June, July, August, with this source also covering October for a second time. The three seasonal monthly names, Winter, Spring and Autumn, are, perhaps, represented by appropriate scenes and figures in January, March and November. However, there are no convincing counterparts for Charlemagne's month-names which are derived from religious festivals: Easter/April and Holy/December. This is consistent with the purely secular themes of the months in the Medieval, but not the Classical artistic tradition.[123] Finally, as we have seen, the picture for June clearly draws upon a Classical source, and five additional

---

[122]) *Un village*: unpaginated frontispiece color plates of fos.124v, 146r, and 96v to Catalogue Nr.108A-C, pp.211-2; Eschweiler, *Der Stuttgarter Bilderpsalter*, pp.116, 129, 140.

[123]) Comet, "Les calendriers", p.36.

months (March, April, July, November and December) seem to exhibit some explicitly Classical influences. From this analysis we may conclude that Swarzenski's argument for the Carolingian originality of these pictures can only be correct with regard to their ensemble and their overall programmatic intent, but certainly not with regard to the specific representations attributed to the individual months, many of which must have had a long history behind them before their appropriation into these manuscripts.

Only September resists all efforts at an iconographic explanation and remains something of a puzzler. The activity depicted, sowing grain, as noted above, is appropriate to the agricultural activities of the month, but it is nearly unparalleled in other pictoral cycles of the "labors" and completely ignores Charlemagne's "Wood-Month" which, presumably, would have been easy to depict by some silvan scene and which may have been shifted totally to November. There is no obvious emendation which would solve this problem. The sowing scene in the mosaic of St Romain-en-Gal is similar, using a basket to hold the seed, and is combined with a plowing scene quite similar to the Salzburg picture for June. It is assigned to late Autumn (November?; see following remarks).[124] The earliest medieval pictoral parallels I can find are for the month of October in two German sources: a Fulda Sacramentary from about 1000 and a 12th-century astronomical table now in Stuttgart.[125] Evidently, this scene reappears regularly for the month of October in the French cycles from the 13th century and is assigned to November in Italian cycles.[126]

In his stimulating essay of 1955, Henri Stern touched on the importance of the *Libri Carolini* for understanding the Salzburg cycle and was the first scholar to introduce Charlemagne's names for the months into the discussion of these pictures. However, for him the argument really turned on a different point. He argued that the only Classical parallel for two of the images in the Salzburg "labors", mowing in July and pasturage and slaughter of pigs in November/December, was the frieze on the surviving 3rd-century Roman arch at Reims.[127] From this he concluded that the, "images des mois carolingiennes s'appuient sur un tradition spécifique de la Gaule romain...[and] ce cycle nouveau semble avoir été créé dans le pays compris entre la Loire et la Belgique...".[128] Indeed, he even suggested that an atelier at the important monastery of St.Amand/Elno or at Corbie might be the place of origin.[129] No doubt there was some Gallic inspiration for these pictures. As we shall see presently, the career of one of its possible patrons, Arn, Archbishop of Salzburg and Abbot of St.Amand, points in that direction. But I think

---

[124]) Stern, "Les calendriers", Pl.XIX, nr 52.

[125]) Webster, *Labors of the Months*, Nrs 28, 89.

[126]) Mane, "Du livre-cathédrale au livre d'heures", p.52.

[127]) "Poesies", p.150; see Table I in his "Les calendriers".

[128]) "Poésies", p.166.

[129]) "Poésies", p.149, n.2, with a cross-reference to Swarzenski.

I. Seasonal Texts and Images

the story is more complex, and there are several obvious problems with Stern's hypothesis.

The image of plowing in June, possibly deriving from a desire to represent Charlemagne's "Fallow-Month", is totally new and is not found in the French cycles although there are later parallels in Germany. Moreover, the following monthly sequence, like that of the month-names, July/Mowing : August/Reaping, in the Salzburg cycle is predominant in the later German cycles and has no parallel in France where, as we have seen, these activities occur a month earlier. Stern's reference to the, apparently West Frankish, poem, "Martius hic falcem", which also describes plowing in June together with haying and harvest in July and August, respectively, is of interest.[130] But the dating is so indeterminate that no firm conclusions about causality, muchless any other sort of relationship, can be drawn from it. Finally, Stern's hypothesis does not address the unique placement of the Salzburg sower in September, and the earliest extant recurrences of this image are in German manuscripts, albeit in the following month, October.

Stern may, indeed, be right in thinking of northeastern France as the most logical homeland for the medieval iconography of the "labors". Nevertheless, the only surviving Carolingian examples of the cycle were generated about as far away as one can get from Stern's putative source and still be within the Frankish Empire, in an area, moreover, which has no special claim to any tradition in seasonal art. And it is extraordinary that not one but two identical manuscripts were produced in a relatively short period, but neither, the original nor the copy, ever left Bavaria! This unexpected and peculiar situation needs to be explained. To me this implies a particularly local interest in the cycle. The existence of the identical copy and the fact that they apparently found no resonance (indeed, surviving depictions of the "labors" only resume in the late tenth century) both indicate that these pictures addressed a specific need at a specific time in a specific place.

My conclusion is that the Salzburg cycle represents a localized "Bavarian" response to some very diverse and cosmopolitan influences. The traces of the contemporary intellectual and artistic interests of the Carolingian Court are prevasive. There is the manuscript context of the revised *computus* which was devised in an "official" royal project in which Charlemagne took a personal interest. Then there are the correspondences to the Codex-Calendar of 354, the *Libri Carolini*, and Charlemagne's month-names which are so heavily quoted in the iconography of the Salzburg cycle that the artist either must have known them himself, or been commissioned by someone who undoubtedly did such as Archbishop Arn.

That the pictures should perpetuate some of the pagan, Classical images implicitly censured by the *Libri Carolini* may reflect the isolation of Theodulf's thinking and the ambivalence which characterizes even his

---

[130]) "Tellurem curvo Junius *proscindit* aratro"; see above for the Roman agricultural writers' use of "proscindere" ("Poésies", pp.144-6: Table on p.149, Text on p.186).

picturae and which produced the copies of the Codex-Calendar of 354. This ambivalence may be contained in the apparently naive readings noted for January and March. But, I think, the explanation may be found, rather, in the purpose behind the pictures as an ensemble, a collective programmatic intent which transformed the significance of the individual pictures. At the beginning of the essay, I indicated that an important motive may have been political. This topic, the political use of the Seasons, was raised first in our discussion of Charlemagne's names for the months. Such considerations were not absent from Carolingian art, at least, in the sense of asserting some broad ideological claim, and the innovative recycling of established Classical models, which characterizes the Salzburg pictures, seems to have been an accepted technique to this end.[131] We also must consider why an identical copy of the Salzburg manuscript was made, possibly, under the influence of the monastery of Mondsee. Finally, how did it find its way from there to the monastery of St Emmeram at Regensburg, the "capital" of the East Frankish Empire? To address these questions more fully we, first, must understand the political situation in Bavaria during the first two decades of the ninth century and the principal personalities involved.

---

[131]) See the interesting recent discussion by Nees, "Carolingian Art and Politics", which concludes that: "Carolingian thinking...is elastic and often multivalent, repeatedly employing familiar concepts and stories...but deploying them in new contexts to carry new messages. Carolingians might in this sense be regarded as postmodernists before their time..." (pp.217-8). It seems to me that this is precisely what the Salzburg artist has done.

II. POLITICAL CONTEXTS AND PERSONALITIES

A. The Carolingian Reconstruction of Bavaria

For much of the eighth century, Bavaria had existed in relative independence under its ruling house, the Agilolfings, who were both related to and rivals of the Arnulfings or Pippinides, later known as the Carolingians. But in 788 Charlemagne finally was able to seize control of the country and depose his allegedly rebellious first cousin, Duke Tassilo. After some evident resistence, which required Charlemagne's continuous presence in Bavaria during 792 and 793, he succeeded in neutralizing fully both Tassilo and his family by the following year, 794.[1] Bavaria then ceased for some time to be a distinct political entity of any importance, and at the *Divisio Regnorum* of 806 it was but one territory amongst others assigned, "as Tassilo had held it [*i.e.* allegedly as a royal benefice] (*sicut Tassilo tenuit*)" by Charlemagne to his son, Pippin.[2]

However, under Charlemagne's son, Louis ["the Pious"], Bavaria's standing appears to have been upgraded systematically. Shortly after Charlemagne's death in 814, Louis despatched (*misit*) his older son and primary heir, Lothar, there to occupy it as his own lordship.[3] In mid-March 815 the Freising episcopal chancery began to style Lothar as King in Bavaria, and in April it referred to "the first year in which...he entered prosperously (*feliciter!*) into Bavaria as King", appellations which continue to occur for almost exactly two years until mid-April 817.[4] Shortly thereafter, in the *Ordinatio imperii* of 817, Bavaria was the core of the territory assigned to Louis' younger son, Ludwig ["the German"], then only about 11 years old.[5] In 826 Ludwig, as

---

[1] This account generally follows Reindel, "Bayern im Karolingerreich", esp.225-36, and "Politische Geschichte Bayerns", esp.pp.249-64. The care that Charlemagne took to eliminate Tassilo is amply demonstrated in: Becher, *Eid und Herrschaft*, pp.21-77; and Laske, "Mönchung Herzog Tassilos". In light of Michael McCormick's recent exposition of the so-called Council of Tegernsee, one wonders whether the final touches were put on the *Libri Carolini* in Regensburg in the summer of 792 ("Textes, images et iconoclasme", pp.133-45).

[2] MGH, Capitularia, vol.1, Nr 45, p.127.

[3] *Annales Regni Francorum, sub anno*, p.141; edition with facing German translation in Rau, *Quellen*, pp.106/7.

[4] Freising, *Traditionen*, Nrs 334/335, p.286 through Nr 372, p.317. The inclusion of Lothar's regnal year seems to be a Freising peculiarity, without counterpart in other Bavarian chanceries, so that it may be reckoned as a personal initiative of the important Bishop Hitto, a member of the leading western Bavarian aristocratic lineage of the Huosi (Störmer, *Früher Adel*, pp.331-2).

[5] "Item Hludowicus volumus ut habeat Baioariam...", MGH, Capitularia, vol.1, Nr 136, p.271. Interestingly, the anonymous "Astronomer's" biography of Louis the Pious ascribes the same term, "despatched" (*misit*; see above), to young Ludwig as the *Annales Regni Francorum* did three years earlier to Lothar ("Hludouuicum in Baioariam misit", Astronomus, *Vita Hludowici imperatoris*, pp.380/1; Rau, *Quellen*, pp.304/5), while the Frankish Royal Annals themselves merely state that he "put him

an adult, was able to enter fully into his rule and was styled as "King" for the first time in Freising documents.[6] By 830 he was designating himself as "divina largiente gratia rex Baioariorum".[7] Regensburg became the effective "capital" of East Francia, and was the site of the only (when modest) mint in the entire realm. Thus, two related developments appear to have been in progress in Bavaria during the early years of the ninth century: first, the integration of Bavaria into the Frankish Empire and, second, the gradual establishment of a new Bavarian "realm" as the core territory of a newly-established East Frankish kingdom.

B. Archbishop Arn of Salzburg

Certainly, the political developments just described were supported by an eccelesiastical one, the elevation of Salzburg to Metropolitan rank by Pope Leo in 798.[8] Salzburg's new status was clearly linked to the pivotal role of its first Archbishop, Arn, who had been the incumbent there as Bishop since 785 and probably owed his institution to Charlemagne. Arn may have fallen into some disfavor with Charlegmagne about the time of Tassilo's deposition in 788.[9] However, he proved himself to be a loyal and useful royal servant in his subsequent efforts to integrate Bavaria into the Carolingian *imperium*. He was the third witness to Charlemagne's will in 811.[10]

Arn's career, personality and interests provide a direct link to Bavaria from the intellectual preoccupations of the Court contained within the *Libri Carolini* and the more parochial interests of Charlemagne which informed the month-names. Although a Bavarian aristocrat by birth and upbringing, Arn had entered the important monastery at St Amand/Elno in the Carolingian heartlands between modern France and Belgium where he became Abbot in 782, a position he continued to hold after his transfer to Salzburg.[11] Thus, we might expect the manuscript culture at Salzburg to exhibit West

---

in charge" there ("Baioariae praefecit", MGH, p.146; Rau, *Quellen*, pp.112/3).

[6] "in ipso anno quo...rex in Baiowaria venit": Freising, *Traditionen*, Nrs 529-538 *passim* (11 March-13 October 826), pp.453-59.

[7] MGH, Diplomata Regum Germaniae, Nr 2, p.2

[8] There is a good, older account in Bauerreiss, *Kirchengeschichte Bayerns*, pp.90-2. The most recent and thorough discussion is by Wavra, *Salzburg und Hamburg*, pp.134-40, who argues that this crucial organizational reform was exclusively a recognition of Arn's close relationship with Charlemagne and that it provoked initial, sturdy resistance from the other Bavarian bishops.

[9] Perhaps, due to the somewhat bizarre effort in 787 by Arn and Abbot Hunrich of Mondsee to enlist, as Tassilo's envoys (*missi*), the mediation of the Pope in the dispute (see the remarks by K.Reindel, "Errichtung einer neuen Bistumsorganisation", p.170, n.4; Becher, *Eid und Herrschaft*, p.59).

[10] Brunner, *Oppositionelle Gruppen*, pp.69ff.

[11] Wolfram, *Geburt Mitteleuropas*, pp.206-16; Platelle, *Le temporel*, pp.53-5. Amandus, Bishop of Maastricht had been a seventh-century missionary to the Slavs of Bavaria (Wolfram, *Ibid.*, p.118).

II. Political Contexts and Personalities

Frankish influences.[12] Moreover, Arn's position as Abbot of St Amand takes us back in the direction of Reims where Stern has localized Classical artistic sources for the "labors" and where the Utrecht Psalter with its incomparably rich rural scenes probably originated.

Arn was an important patron of learning. His entry under 24 January [821] in the twelfth-century Necrology of St.Rupert, Salzburg, notes that "amongst other innumerable and laudable works, he caused 150 volumes to be assembled here" (? *conscribi*, possibly, "written").[13] He was a friend and protege of Alcuin, with whom he conducted a voluminous correspondence, and a participant in the intellectual and cultural activities of the Carolingian Court so that those preoccupations, as well, should be represented in the works of the Salzburg *scriptorium*.[14] One of Arn's first actions in 798 as the new Bavarian metropolitan was to regulate the observance of church festivals at the provincial council of Reisbach.[15] From every point of view he is the most likely candidate for patronage of the Salzburg manuscript.[16] But, did he act alone, and do these pictures represent solely his personal interests? We must return to the political history of Bavaria and the persons of its governors to consider this question.

C. Sheriff Audulf in Bavaria

During the last decade of the eighth century and most of the first two decades of the ninth, Bavaria was governed directly by the Frankish Crown through Imperial Legates, designated most commonly as "Sheriffs" (or "Ealdormen"; *comites*) and occasionally referred to in the Roman style as "Prefects".[17] These governors not only exercised an important military role on the Bavarian frontiers with the various Slavic peoples but also participated in internal civil matters, sitting, for example, as royal Commissioners or *missi* at court sessions and inquests together with senior churchmen, and attending church assemblies.

Because of the need for the Emperor's personal confidence in them, the more

---

[12]) Bischoff, *Schreibschulen* II, pp.61-73.

[13]) MGH, Necrologia Germanie, vol.2, p.61.

[14]) Fleckenstein notes, for example, that a former student of Alcuin at the Court school, Aldrich, also studied with Arn and served as his chaplain in Salzburg. *Hofkapelle* 1, p.71; *cf*.also Bischoff, *Schreibschulen* II, p.61, n.32, for Wizo-Candidus.

[15]) See von Finckenstein, "Fest- und Feiertage", p.123.

[16]) We should note here one small apparent anomoly, that Codex 387 was executed in the last successor to an indigenous Salzburg hand (Stil II), not in the West Frankish influenced hand imported from St.Amand under Arn (Bischoff, *Schreibschulen* II, pp.72-3 [Arn-Stil]).

[17]) In Einhard's words: "...neque provincia, quam tenebat [Tassilo], ulterius duci, sed comitibus ad regendum commissa est." (*Vita Karoli Magni*, c.11, MGH, p.14; Rau, Quellen, pp.180/1). Full discussions in: Mitterauer, *Karolingische Markgrafen*, pp.1-84; Brunner, "Fränkische Fürstentitel", pp.235-8; Bowlus, *Franks, Moravians and Magyars*, pp.46-89. For the Roman office of Prefect see discussion by K.Dietz in *Römer in Bayern*, pp.55-8.

important figures were drawn necessarily from the highest ranks of the "Imperial Aristocracy" (Reichsaristokratie) and often were persons of some prominence at the royal Court.[18] The first, the "Prefect" Gerold (from 791), was killed under somewhat unusual circumstances on a military expedition in Pannonia in 799. He was the brother of Charlemagne's consort, Hildegard, and a patron of the Reichenau. Significantly, as we shall see presently, Gerold also could trace his descent from the same branch of the Agilolfings as the deposed Bavarian ducal family.[19] The second was the royal Seneschall, Audulf, who is only referred to as "comes" or "missus", never as "prefect".[20] He enjoyed an exceptionally long imcumbency of almost 20 years (799-818) during the crucial period just described, bridging the reigns of Charlemagne and Louis the Pious through to the disposition of the Ordinatio imperii of 817.

Audulf was certainly a key participant, perhaps, even the prime architect in the political reconstruction of Bavaria. His services evidently were recognized and endorsed by the Emperor Louis, since, despite Audulf's apparent membership in Charlemagne's "Old Guard", he was continued in office after the latter's death. The fullness of Audulf's authority was acknowledged in a posthumous Freising document of 30 December 819 dictated by Bishop Hitto of Freising and issued on behalf of his widow and son of the same name while they all were at Aachen.[21] This exceptional eulogy, undoubtedly drafted with an eye to cultivation of royal favor for his widow and son, testified, "how Audulf received the very same authority over the country of the

---

[18]) Still fundamental to this discussion is Tellenbach's classic, Königtum und Stämme, esp.pp.14-18. There is now a good review of the Carolingian "Reichsaristokratie" in English by Airlie, "The aristocracy".

[19]) Werner, "Bedeutende Adelsfamilien", pp.111-2; Jarnut, "Genealogie und politische Bedeutung", pp.17, 21.

[20]) There is a very useful biographical sketch of Audulf in: Schreibmüller, "Audulf"; Wolfram, Geburt Mitteleuropas, pp.194-5; Annales Regni Francorum, sub anno (MGH, p.72; Rau, Quellen, pp.48/9-50/1), where Audulf is called "miss[us] su[us]" and "sinescalc[us]". Ever since Schreibmüller's study, Audulf also has been attributed comital office in the Frankish Taubergau ("Audulf", esp.pp.53-4, 60-1; Schulze, Grafschaftsverfassung, p.230), but I believe this is incorrect. The reference in an Imperial diploma of 807 "in ipso comitatu Audolfi" in the Taubergau seems, rather, to be connected to his comital "benefiti[um]" there than to any office (MGH, Diplomata Karolinorum, vol.1, Nr 206, pp.275-6;

see the Mittellateinisches Wörterbuch, col.925, def.IIA, 1b, sub verbo). The original diploma, formerly Bayerisches Hauptstaatsarchiv, Munich, Kaiserselekt 3, has been transferred to the Staatsarchiv Würzburg, Urkunde 1203, but I was able to examine a photocopy in Munich. Audulf evidently also held a benefice in Brittany, probably a result of his successful leadership as "missus" of a campaign against the Bretons in 786 (Schreibmüller, "Audulf", pp.63-4).

[21]) "Ego Tagabertus scripsi iussione domini Hittonis episcopi", Freising, Traditionen, Nr 397c, pp.338-9. Audulf died in the same year as Archibishop Hildebald of Cologne, in very late 818 or early 819 (Annales S.Emmerammi Ratisponensis Maiores, p.93, sub anno "819"; Schreibmüller, "Audulf", p.62). See below.

II. Political Contexts and Personalities

Bavarians in full measure and with honor from the pious Emperor Carl and thereafter also from Louis to supervise, rule and govern this country".[22]

Audulf's family background has never been elucidated fully, a task which might be impossible.[23] He was a Frank and seems, like his predecessor, Gerold, to have had connections to the Middle Rhine country between Mainz and Worms.[24] This area has also been recognized as the homeland of one important branch of the Agilolfing family to which Gerold, almost certainly, and Audulf, possibly, had connections.[25] As the testimony above indicates, Audulf (in contrast to Gerold) evidently struck deep roots in Bavaria during his long tenure, surely aided by the local connections of his widow, who must have been a remarkable person in her own right. Her unusual name, in its Bavarian form, "Keyla/Keilana", is apparently of Langobard origin ("Geila"), and may itself be programmatic, since it was born by an early seventh-century daughter of Duke Gisulf of Friaul, who was abducted by the Avars and ransomed back, subsequently to marry a "princeps Baivariorum".[26] Keila's family, like

---

[22]) *Loc.cit.*: "...quomodo Audulfus super provincia Baiowariorum tam potenter et honorabiliter a pio imperatore Karolo, deinde etiam a Hluduwico eandem potestatem accepit hanc provinciam praevidere regere et gubernare...". The use of "regere", in particular, to describe Audulf's power is an indication of his importance and may even echo the quasi-royal position of the Agilolfing Dukes of Bavaria (See below for the discussion in Section II.F).

[23]) Schreibmüller, "Audulf", pp.62-8.

[24]) The Middle Rhenish connections of Gerold and related persons have been examined extensively, if not always conclusively, by Gockel, *Karolingische Königshöfe*, pp.238-56, 275-94, 307-10; and by Staab, *Untersuchungen*, pp.380-401. The Bavarian genealogical connections of these Middle Rhenish groups are discussed most recently by Hamann, "Frühe genealogische Verbindungen", pp.64-9. None of them mentions Audulf, but it is worth considering that an Audulf and a Gerold both held land in [Erbes]büdesheim in the Wormsgau which they donated to the monastery of Lorsch in 767/8 and 771, respectively. This Gerold was married at that time to an *Aut*-lind (Lorsch, *Codex*, vol.2, Nrs 1891-2, p.477); an Autolf, married to an Odolsvint, also occurs in 769 in the Kreichgau (*ibid.*, vol.3, Nr 2228, p.8). For this Audulf see: Wenskus, *Sächsischer Stammesadel*, pp.98-100, 109-10, 317.

[25]) "Im Mittelrheingebiet zwischen Mainz und Worms wird man also für das 7./8. Jahrhundert einen Schwerpunkt der agilolfingischen Sippenmacht sehen dürfen." (Störmer, "Herzogsgeschlecht", pp.147-8. Friese, *Studien*, pp.51-3, 68-76.

[26]) Friese, *Studien*, pp.38-40. The impressive but somewhat picaresque story of Geila and her siblings was recounted at length by Paul the Deacon and undoubtedly represents an oral tradition carefully preserved by her descendants (Paul the Deacon, *Historia Langobardorum*, Book IV, Chapter 37, pp.128-31; Foulke, pp.179-84). For comment on the incident see Jarnut, *Prosopographische und sozialgeschichtliche Studien*, *sub* "LXI. Gisulfus II", pp.354-5; and on the Agilolfing onomastic connections of the names in Gaila's family see Wagner, "Zur Herkunft", pp.36-41. Our Keyla experienced the final demise of Avar power in the early ninth century after a series of major campaigns, one of

that of Archbishop Arn, seems to have had an important center of its property and influence in the Sempt-Isen region of Bavaria south of Freising.[27] She evidently formed a strong relationship with Bishop Hitto of Freising, and after Audulf's death she "remained" in Bavaria along with her (evidently still young) son, also named Audulf, a sure sign of her local affinities but, perhaps, also an acknowledgement of her ultimate origins elsewhere.[28]

Audulf had no fixed "capital" from which he could exercise a sedentary authority, but he does seem to be linked especially to the old *Agilolfing* ducal residence at Regensburg, certainly the most important urban settlement in Bavaria at this time.[29] His governance of Bavaria must be considered in association with the activities of Archibishop Arn of Salzburg. In all five of the Freising deeds covering the years 802 to, perhaps, as late as 811 where Audulf occurs in various administrative and judicial capacities, he acts in association with Arn, and in the first four

---

which in 799 had cost the life of the Prefect Gerold. There is no evidence that her husband, Audulf, was active in these campaigns although, together with his colleague, Werner, he did lead the Bavarian contingent in a major expedition against Bohemia in 805/6 (Schreibmüller, "Audulf", p.57).

[27]) For Keyla's Sempt-Isen connections see: Sturm, *Anfänge*, pp.205-6, and *cf*.pp.82-104, for other families, including Arn's, from this area. Michael Mitterauer and Gottfried Mayr both have identified Keyla with a daughter of the "Mainz" magnate, Otakar, who may have been linked to the foundation of the important Bavarian monastery of Tegernsee (Mitterauer, *Karolingische Markgrafen*, pp.57-8; Mayr, *Studien*, p.145; there is a short review of the various and not always transparent attributions of "Otakar" in Störmer, *Früher Adel*, esp.pp.97-8). However, the investigations of Michael Gockel (*Karolingische Königshöfe*, p.248) and Franz Staab (*Untersuchungen*, p.382) do not seem to sustain this connection. An argument for Keyla's Sempt-Isen connections is the fact that in 818 her former slave, Engilpoto, purchased property near Erding for presentation to Freising and had the transaction witnessed a second time at Isen (see below).

[28]) "...coniux eius Keyla remansit in Baiowaria simul cum eius filio Audulfo iuvene", Freising,

---

Traditionen, Nr 397c, p.338. Keyla's good relationship to Bishop Hitto of Freising is evident in the tribute to Audulf at the beginning of this deed and also in her close association with Hitto at the Imperial Palace in Aachen where this deed was witnessed ("Pergenti vero pio pontifice Hittoni ad palacium iubente et vocante domino imperatore...et Keyla simulque aderat et Audulfus [the son]..." Audulf's filial homonym either died early or did not have a distinguished career. Perhaps, he is the "Otolt" who occurs regularly as Bishop Hitto's Lay Steward (*advocatus*) from 826 onwards (Freising, *Traditionen*, Nr 538a, p.459).

[29]) In 802 Audulf presided with other *missi* at a royal court-session (*placitum*) held in Regensburg which is referred to as a "civita[s] publica" (Freising, *Traditionen*, Nr 183, p.174). See, however, the famous Capitulary of Diedenhofen/Thionville from 805 where Audulf, exceptionally, is responsible (*praevideat*) for two centers in addition to Regensburg, reaching as far north into Franconia as Forchheim on the Regnitz River, from which to control the illicit arms trade with the Slavic East (MGH, Capitularia, vol.1, Nr 44, c.7, p.123; perhaps this is the basis for his comital benefice in the Taubergau). By contrast, his eastern counterpart, Werner, had only Linz.

II. Political Contexts and Personalities

documents Arn leads in order of precedence.[30]

Indeed, there may be some special circumstances and even some tensions surrounding this documentary evidence. Recently, it has been argued, largely on formalistic, diplomatic evidence, that as part of the reform movement initiated by the *Capitulare missorum generale* in the Spring of 802 Arn attempted to establish a new *missaticum* in Bavaria under his authority.[31] Since the capitulary is to a large degree concerned with improving the standards of justice, it is tempting to link this development to a remarkable letter of 13 April from Alcuin to Arn where Alcuin urges Arn to proclaim to Word of Life often to "our friend of old, Audulf" so that "he might be just in his judgments and merciful to the poor" and thereby secure heavenly protection, "lest, he place himself unprepared in peril, as his predecessors who met a violent death".[32] This is very strong language and a clear reference to the death of Audulf's predecessor, Gerold, in 799 and, possibly, to that of Sheriff Goteram of the Traungau in 802. Such a veiled threat went far beyond the conventions and formulaic exhortations which are commonplace in such correspondence. Perhaps, its implied charge forms the pretext upon which Arn attempted to assert his primacy in missatical jurisdiction. In any event, Audulf appears to have outlasted any challenge, since, in the last two Bavarian documents where both appear, dated between 807 and 811, Audulf is designated a "missus" and Arn bears only his ecclesiastical title.[33]

---

[30]) Freising, *Traditionen*, Nrs 183, 227, 231, 242, and 247, pp.174, 210-1, 213-4, 221 and 223-4. The only reference to Audulf in the other Bavarian cartularies, which are much inferior to that of Freising in completeness of coverage, is in a Regensburg deed of 14 September 808 where he occurs without Arn (Regensburg, *Traditionen*, Nr 10, p.9).

[31]) Goldberg, "Dilectissimus Pater". Mr Goldberg kindly discussed this interesting work with me and provided relevant excerpts. There is some preliminary comment on Goldberg's hypothesis by Wolfram in his *Salzburg, Bayern, Österreich*, pp.185-8.

[32]) "...praedicet Odulfo nostro olim amico verbum vitae saepius, ut sit iustus in iudiciis, et misericors in pauperes...Nec se inconsulte tradat periculis, quomodo quidam antecessores sui fecerunt, et ideo inproba morte perierunt." (Alcuin, *Epistolae*, Nr 264, pp.421-2). Dümmler dates the letter provisionally to 803. The word "olim" used to describe their relationship to Audulf is ambiguous and could mean either "former" or "long-time" (Schreibmüller, "Audulf", pp.58-9). An "Aotolfus" occurs in a property list from the monastery of Niederalteich as having despoiled it (*nobis abstulit*) of two properties (*Breviarius Urolfi*, pp.60-96, esp.pp.90/1). Although the "Breviarius" seems to date from about 790, it is not clear that this section (III), which the editor does not consider in his discussion of the document's structure (pp.75-82), is integral to the preceeding sections and could be a later addition; Abbot Urolf remained in office until 814. The alienated property apparently was located in an isolated position, "Leuuir"/Lebern (LK Altötting), 76 km southwest of Niederalteich, and lay somewhat to the east of Keyla's Sempt-Isen homeland.

[33]) Freising, *Traditionen*, Nrs 242, 247, pp.221, 224; in the latter document Audulf asserts authority over two other royal officials: "Tunc iussit Audulfus Job comite et Ellanberto iudice, ut hoc

It is not surprising that two men, each possessing such outstanding abilities and personal dynamism, should experience some friction in their dealings with one another. Their careers in Bavaria were intertwined, and the conclusion to this particular episode seems to have been more in the nature of a mutual truce, since Audulf himself, like Arn, soon recedes from the surviving documentation of routine administration. For the last decade or so of his incumbency until his death, there is a dearth of direct evidence about his whereabouts and activities.[34] Their last appearance together was in 811 as witnesses to Charlemagne's testament, surely an indication that the Emperor had confidence in their ability to cooperate for the promotion of his interests.[35]

There is one final piece of deed evidence that must be considered in our assessment of Audulf. It relates to his last documented appearance in April 818, shortly before his death.[36] This deed contains an account of how "a certain layman by the name of Engilpoto" bought a piece of property from a noblewoman and her son and then donated it to the cathedral church of Freising. Both of these activities were part of everyday conveyancing in Carolingian Bavaria.[37] However, there are three items of particular interest here. First, there is the identity of Engilpoto himself who turns out to be a former slave of Audulf's wife, Keyla, manumitted and commended by her at some time to Bishop Hitto.[38] Second, we learn in the following year after Audulf's death that he himself had been present at this double transaction in 818 along with many other Bavarian worthies even though his name does not appear on the witness list.[39] Third, the transaction of April

---

caute et sollicite inquirerent" in their oathtaking. Dating emendations proposed in Goldberg, "Dilectissimus Pater", Table 3, p.92, who concludes, "What we seem to be witnessing...after 807...is the shift from Arn to Audulf as the chief *missus* in Bavaria" (p.82).

[34]) Goldberg argues that Arn's advanced age explains his apparent retirement from active public affairs, which is consistent with the thrust of Wolfram's account ("Dilectissimus Pater", p.82; *Geburt Mitteleuropas*, p.209). We have no direct evidence of Audulf's age, but he too may well have been advanced in years at this time. It is possible that during Lothar's two year direct tenure in Bavaria from March 815 to April 817 (see above) some of Audulf's authority was suspended and his duties temporarily attenuated.

[35]) Einhard, *Vita Karoli Magni* (MGH, p.41; Rau, Quellen, pp.210-1). Brunner, *Oppositionelle Gruppen*, pp.66, 79.

[36]) Freising, Traditionen, Nr.397a, p.337.

[37]) See my "Land Sales", p72.

[38]) "proprium servum illius Engilpoto nomine...in fide et caritate commendavit...illum liberum dimissum pro redemptionem anime suae habuisset", Freising, *Traditionen*, Nr 397c, p.338. This probably explains why the transaction subsequently had to be repeated in front of the widow and son at Aachen "aliter firmum esse non valuisset". Some degree of dependency on the former master continued to inhere in a manumitted slave, and Engilpoto's title to property previously acquired may not have been clear.

[39]) *Loc.cit*.: "Et legitima emptione et traditione inter eos act et confirmata coram Audulfo et multis aliis in Baioaria honoratis" which must refer to Audulf

II. Political Contexts and Personalities

818 was witnessed in the first instance by "Egilolfus pedagogus Hloduwici iuvenis".[40]

Both Engilpoto and Egilolf deserve closer attention. Regarding Engilpoto, the most likely account is that he had displayed unusual talent; had served his mistress' husband, Audulf, well; had achieved, thereby, some form of privileged status and prosperity; and after Audulf's death had been manumitted as a reward.[41] Certainly, we must assume some extraordinary position to explain the presence of Audulf, Egilolf, the king's educator, and numerous Bavarian dignitaries at a routine property transaction. The only other mention of an Engilpoto in the contemporary deed evidence occurs during the first year of the Emperor Louis' reign in August 814 when an "Engilpoto missus dominicus" follows a "Liutpald comes" and precedes a "Deothart vicarius dominicus" as the first three witnesses to property transaction involving Bishop Hitto of Freising.[42] Sheriff Liutpald is the second witness following the "pedagogus" Egilolf to Engilpoto's donation in 818, and if we did not possess the deed of 819 designating Engilpoto as a former slave, we would not hesitate to identify the "missus dominicus" of 814 with the Freising benefactor of 818. However we may wish to resolve this particular issue, it suggests to me that in the later period of his office Audulf did not lack agents of his authority, both recognized officials in subordinate positions like Sheriffs Liutpald and, possibly, Job who served, respectively, as witnesses to Engilpoto's two original deeds, and even through individuals such as Engilpoto, personally dependent on him and his family.[43]

Senior and to Freising, *Traditionen*, Nr 397a, since Audulf Junior as a "iuven[is]" always occurs together with his mother, and only in 818 is there a double transaction.

[40]) Störmer thought that Freising, *Traditionen*, Nr 397a might have been executed at Aachen like Nr 397c because of Egilolf's presence (*Früher Adel*, p.76). This is a plausible suggestion, but since Nr 397a was executed on 18 April and was "renewed" only eight days later on 26 April in Bavaria at Isen, I think it is more likely that the original transaction witnessed by Audulf took place at the site of the property itself at Kinzlbach near Erding which lies between Freising and Isen. It is worth noting that the term "pedagogus" had servile connotations in Classical Latin.

[41]) It is always possible that Engilpoto was Audulf's slave who had passed to Keyla as part of his estate, but one would then expect Audulf to be mentioned in the act of piety at his manumission.

[42]) Freising, *Tradtionen*, Nr 320, p.274. This is the first deed in the Freising cartulary dated according to Louis' regnal year, and one may think in this context of Louis promotion of the career of Archbishop Ebbo of Rheims, a former royal slave. Before the reforms of 802, *missi* were routinely recruited from amongst relatively modest retainers and vassals, of whom the latter still bore certain connotations of servility (see the recent remarks by Fleckenstein, "Missus/missaticum").

[43]) The evidence, of course, is circumstantial. Liutpald first appears in the Bavarian evidence as a "comes" in 806-8, just at the time of Audulf's last securely documented appearances, and seems to be active continuously for almost four decades (Freising, *Traditionen*, Nrs 235/6, pp.217-8ff). Despite the intense documentation, his origins are uncertain. Job on the other hand comes from the well-known clan bearing Biblical names which was centered in the Sempt-Isen

Egilolf, the royal educator, on the other hand, may have been related to Audulf.[44] He bears a name which is prominant in the Middle Rhine, the probable homeland of Gerold and Audulf, and which had became the "Leading Name" (*Leitname*) of the Agilolfings even though it never occurs amongst the surviving references to the Bavarian rulers of that family.[45] In the imperial diploma of 807 where Audulf's link to the Frankish Taubergau is revealed, Audulf was engaged in an exchange of land with the Bishop of Würzburg where, for his part, he handed over property which a "Hundulf formerly was deemed to hold within Audulf's comital benefice and which his son, the priest, Agilulf, is deemed to hold up to now".[46] The common final name-element, "-ulf" is suggestive of a relationship as is the property link.[47] Josef Sturm, on the other hand, proposed a Bavarian Egilolf whose family was established in the same area as Keyla and Arn which would indicate a different route of connection but the same result.[48]

These excursions regarding Engilpoto and Egilolf, both suggest that Audulf continued to be discretely active in his efforts to "supervise, rule and govern effectively and honorably over the land of the Bavarians". And we may suspect that this role included influencing the formation of its new ruler, the young Ludwig during the first year or so of his Bavarian minority from 817, through the choice of a suitable praeceptor.[49] Moreover, it

---

region and may have been related to Keyla (Sturm, *Anfänge*, p.90; see above).

[44]) For Egilolf see the interesting but, perhaps, somewhat excessive remarks in Friese, *Studien*, pp.68-9.

[45]) See Gockel, *Karolingische Königshöfe*, esp.pp.289-93, and *cf.* Staab, *Untersuchungen*, esp.p.398, for other significant occurences of Aglilofing name material.

[46]) "...Hundulfus quondam in ipso comitatu Audolfi visus fuit habere et filius eius Agilulfus presbiter adhuc habere visus est" (MGH, Diplomata Karolinorum, vol.1, Nr 206, p.276). See above for a discussion of Audulf's "comitat[us]". In 832 Einhart wrote on terms of familiarity to an Egilolf and a *Hun*-bert seeking the continuation of a benefice which his retainer (*homini nostro*), Gerbert, had received from the Bishop of Würzburg in the Taubergau (Einhard, *Epistolae*, Nr 24, pp.121-2). An Egilolf, his son [*sic*] Helpfolf, his brother Huswart, and his father Huntolf, all occur in two Fulda deeds at the end of the eighth century, both witnessed by an Einhart (Fulda, *Urkundenbuch*, Nrs 200-01, pp.296-9; *cf.ibid.*, Nrs 427 and 528, pp.471, 507-8). For this Hundulf, father of Agilulf the priest, see Gockel, *Karolingische Königshöfe*, pp.63, 278-9. It should be remembered that Einhart himself was married to an Imma and, thus, may have had an affinity with the Prefect Gerold and, perhaps, even with Audulf. The importance of Imma is discussed in the forthcoming article by Wilhelm Störmer, "Einhards Herkunft", which he kindly provided to me in manuscript. *Cf.*the differing commentary on Egilolf in Bosl, *Franken um 800*, pp.70-1.

[47]) Schreibmüller, "Audulf", p.60.

[48]) *Anfänge*, p.206. Given the mobility of the Carolingian aristocracy, these positions are, of course, not necessarily exclusive.

[49]) It is interesting to contemplate a Carolingian being tutored by an "Agilolfing" in preparation for his assumption of royal power in Bavaria!

appears that Audulf and his family enjoyed a close and cooperative relationship with Hitto, the prominent Bishop of Freising since 811 and a member of the powerful western Bavarian *genealogia* of the Huosi, whose episcopal chancery, we noted above, was particularly zealous in recognizing shifts in Bavaria's political leadership. I also believe that Audulf also was a crucial figure in the introduction of the "labors of the months" into Bavaria.

D. Audulf and Court Culture

As royal Seneschall, the senior Court official charged with oversight of the King's food and other domestic affairs, Audulf was an important figure in the Court hierarchy and society.[50] Unlike his predecessor Gerold, he also participated in the cultural activities and conceits of the Court. Many of the important figures at Charlemagne's Court bore learned pseudonyms.[51] We already have noted Archbishop Arn's: *Aquila*, the "Eagle". But not all were so obvious. Audulf was referred to as, "Menalcas" and was depicted in three important poems dedicated to Charlemagne by Court *literati*. Alcuin greets the other principal Court official, the royal Chamberlain, Meginfrid, and Audulf with the wish that "Thyrsis [Meginfrid] may always prosper and also Menalcas", and then humorously describes Audulf in his office as Senschall, "personally (*ipse*) chastising the cooks in the blackened kitchen hall/so that Flaccus [Alcuin] might have warm gruel by the bowlful (*calidos...per fercula pultes*)".[52] Angilbert, the Abbot of S.Riquier, likewise shows Audulf in facetious but somewhat more literary guise, perhaps playing upon the ruddy face of a cook: "Menalcas shall descend, soaked through [*uvidus*:drunk?] from the rainy peak [*Regens*-burg?]/so that he might read these verses worthily out of love to the great hall of the Palace (? *aulae condignus amore*)./Worthy love for the poets suffuses the heart of Menalcas with a ruddy glow"(*Dignus amor rutilat vatorum in corde Menalce*).[53] And the Archchaplain, Theodulf, primary author of the *Libri Carolini*, reverts to a mild burlesque of Audulf's office: "Let shrewd (*sollers*) Menalcas approach from his fertile abode (*Pomiflua..de sede*),/wiping sweat with his hand from the top of his brow./As often as he sets to the task (*ingrediens*), surrounded by troops of bakers and cooks, he presides over the assembly/sauce (*ius synodale gerit*)./He who performs all things wisely, let him bear the

---

[50]) Fleckenstein, "Karl der Große und sein Hof", pp.32-3; Brühl, *Fodrum, Gistum, Servitium Regis*, pp.77-8, 378 n.124.

[51]) Fleckenstein, "Karl der Große und sein Hof", pp.43-6; and *idem*, "Alcuin", pp.18-21.

[52]) Alcuin, *Carmina*, Nr 26, p.246. This and the following are my translations. Both Latin text and English translations are found in Godman's excellent, *Poetry*, pp.120/1. We may see the influence of this and the other mild burlesques of Audulf in the somewhat later *Chronicon* of Abbot Regino of Prüm, Audulf is designated "princ[eps] cocorum" (p.55)!

[53]) Angilbert, *Carmina*, Nr 2, p.362; Godman, *Poetry*, pp.116/7. For "Regensburg" see Schreibmüller, "Audulf", p.56, based upon a suggestion by von Simson.

banquet feast before the honored royal throne".[54]

Angilbert's poem suggests that Audulf may have participated himself in Court literary exercises. In another poem, Theodulf seems to support this in a somewhat obscure allusion to Menalcas' sharp tongue and his aptness in literary contests: "From his smokey mouth (*fumoso ore*) in song and verse/He sang this to us, behold, Menalcas/Dead with exhaustion (*Exanimis*) skewered the living by sharp mockery (*risu percussit iniquo*)./Nevertheless, these contests (*praelia*) are profitable for the lads."[55] Indeed, Alcuin may have preserved a poem by Audulf/Menalcas, a somewhat pedestrian lament for the absence of a mutual friend bearing the pseudonym "Cuculus", the Cuckoo, who was evidently forced to return to England by a malicious step-mother (*saeva noverca*).[56] It is notable for us only because of its allusions to Virgil's fifth *Eclogue* and its play on seasonal imagery, particularly the cuckoo's hoped-for return in the Spring (*Non pereat cuculus, veniet sub tempore veris,/Et nobis veniens carmina laeta ciet*).

The literary connections attributed to Audulf, including the implied intimacy of their humor, are extraordinary and stand in sharp contrast to the relative artistic silence surrounding his predecessor, Gerold, despite the latter's possibly higher social status, his certain renown as a warrior, and his extraordinarily powerful political connections.[57] I would argue that these conceits should be taken seriously as clues to Audulf's character and interests. In particular, the origin of the the pseudonym, "Menalcas", is worth some consideration because these "found" names were certainly in some way programmatic or descriptive of their bearers, as Charlemagne's, "David", clearly was. Both Angilbert and Theodulf echo the literary source of the figure, Menalcas: Virgil's tenth *Eclogue*, where "The shepherd approached, followed tardily by the swineherds./Menalcas approached soaked through from the winter's mast."[58] Thus, the figure of Menalcas places us clearly in the world of rural pastimes and seasonal activities described by bucolic verse.

But, it is Virgil's third *Eclogue* that brings us precisely (and finally) back to the realm of the calendar and the seasons. This *Eclogue*, patterned after the (now considered spurious) eighth *Idyll* of Theocritus, the originator of the genre, depicts a song contest between two rustics, Menalcas and Damoetus (the pseudonym for Riculf, Archbishop of Mainz!). Menalcas stakes his most valuable possessions, two beechwood cups, the "work of divine Alcimedon" upon which are carved

---

[54]) Theodulf, *Carmina*, Nr 25, p.488; Godman, *Poetry*, pp.158/9. For the pun on "ius" see Schreibmüller, "Audulf", p.57.

[55]) Theodulf, *Carmina*, Nr 27, p.492.

[56]) Alcuin, *Carmina*, Nr 57, pp.269-70. Schreibmüller argues that vv.5-52 following, "Incipe tu senior, quaeso, Menalca prior" should be attributed to the figure Menalcas/Audulf ("Audulf", p.52). However, we should be mindful of the inherent ambiguities of the literary *personae* in all of this verse.

[57]) See the remarks on Gerold by Ross, "Two Neglected Paladins", p.234.

[58]) *Ecloga* X, vv.19-20, pp.72/3.

II. Political Contexts and Personalities

within "spreading clusters of pale ivy" two figures, one named, the Samian mathematician and astronomer, Conon, and: "Who was the other one?/The one who described with his compass (*descripsit radio*) the whole circle of the heavens (*orbem*) for man,/which seasons the harvester should keep and which the plowman, bent at his curved blade?"[59]

The image on the cups is completely different from the attractive genre scenes which characterize Virgil's apparent immediate inspiration in Theocritus' first *Idyll* (vv.27-59) or, indeed, the ultimate source of both, "The Shield of Achilles" in Homer's *Illiad* (Bk XVIII, vv.478-608). The reference to "the other one" recalls, rather specifically, a seminal passage in Hesiod's *Works and Days*: "When the Pleiades, the daughters of Atlas, rise, begin your reaping; your ploughing, when they set" (vv.383-4). Thus, the most singular defining characteristic of Virgil's Menalcas is the possession of an artistic object, embedded firmly within the astronomical learning of Antiquity, which recalls the seasonal activities of the country calendar and links the world of necessary human activity to the course of natural events! Moreover, within the serious playfulness of these Court literary conventions, Charlemagne himself, the namer of the months and their labors, passionate student of astronomy, and patron of the *computus*, may have been inferred as the unnamed person who harmonizes the heavens and the earth. In any event, the Emperor himself was certainly linked to this third *Eclogue* by Alcuin who, in his seasonal poem, a debate between Spring and Winter, refers to Charlemagne under the pseudonym Palaemon, the judge of the contest between Menalcas and Damoetus.[60] Therefore, the Bavarian Prefect, Audulf, emerges as a powerful figure who incorporated both a purposeful political agenda and a clear identification with seasonal art and calendrical matters.[61]

E. Archbishop Hildebald and Bishop Baturich

If Arn can be assigned the patronage for Codex 387, are there significant personal associations for the manuscript copy, Clm 210, as well? It was noted above that the manuscript exhibits clear influences of a hand characteristic of the monastery of Mondsee. Mondsee, located somewhat to the east-northeast of Salzburg, maintained, possibly, the most important *scriptorium* in Carolingian Bavaria.[62] Founded by Duke Tassilo, it occupied an important position in Bavaria as indicated by the fact that its Abbot, Hunric,

---

[59]) *Ecloga* III, vv.37-42, pp.18/9. There are several candidates for "the other one" but no definitive solution. Indeed, the very vagueness of the allusion may be part of Menalcas' bumpkin *persona*! See Clausen, *Commentary*, pp.100-3.

[60]) Alcuin, *Carmina*, "Conflictus Veris et Hiemis", pp.270-2; text and English translation in Godman, *Poetry*, pp.145/6-8/9: *cf*.Godman, *Poets and Emperors*, p.79, for the appropriation of this figure, Palaemon, by Moduin of Autun.

[61]) Presumably, the Carolingians did not dwell upon Menalcas' sexual preferences which are declared in the course of the third *Eclogue*.

[62]) Bischoff, *Schreibschulen* II, pp.9-16; Wolfram, *Geburt Mitteleuropas*, pp.227-32.

was Arn's companion on the quixotic mission to Rome in 787 which attempted to reconcile Charlemagne and Tassilo.

Mondsee maintained its importance under the new regime. In 803 it was impropriated to Hildebald, Archbishop of Cologne, the head of the Chapel Royal from 791 until his death at about the same time as Audulf in 818/9.[63] As a leading royal servant, he was well acquainted with Archbishop Arn. In 799, together with Arn, he headed the Imperial Commission to Rome which investigated the charges against Pope Leo III and which prepared the way for the subsequent coronation of Charlemagne.[64] He was the first witness to Charlemagne's will and carried the Court pseudonym "Aaron".[65] Finally, Hildebald may have been related to the aristocratic Bavarian clan which founded the monastery at Schliersee in the later years of Agilolfing rule (before 779) and which, apparently, had important connections to the founders of Tegernsee and to the Middle Rhine region.[66]

Hildebald is well known as the rebuilder of Cologne cathedral, as a collector of precious artifacts, as the patron by 805 of an important *computus* manuscript and, possibly, as the person who patronized the copying of the *Liber pontificalis*.[67] There is direct evidence of

---

[63]) He may never have been formally "Abbot", and his normal duties were evidently discharged by a certain deacon, Lantperht, who is first designated as Abbot in 816 and remained so until his death, possibly in October 829: Fleckenstein, *Hofkapelle* 1, pp.49-52; article by Wisplinghoff, in the *Neue Deutsche Biographie*, vol.9, p.118; Mondsee, *Traditionsbuch*, pp.70-72. The name of Hildebald's deacon and commissioner (*missus*), Lantperht, indicates that he too may have belonged to the mighty Bavarian lineage (*genealogia*) of the Huosi with direct connections to the West Frankish bishoprics of Auxerre and Langres. See Störmer, *Adelsgruppen*, pp.105-8, esp.107; but *cf.*Mondsee, *Traditionsbuch*, p.72, n.52. The chronology of Hildebald's career implies that his protege (and relative ?), Lantperht, could have been responsible for the production of Clm 210. Lantperht was certainly a patron of learning, but Hildebald's influence as a prominent Court official, colleague of Archbishop Arn, and patron of the arts must have played a role as well.

[64]) The delegation also included Bishop Atto of Freising, who, like his successor, Hitto, was a member of the *genealogia* of the Huosi. See the account in Leo III's biography (Nr 98) in the "Liber Pontificalis": *Le Liber Pontificalis*, pp.6-7; English translation with commentary in Davis, *Lives*, p.189; Folz, *Coronation*, pp.132-3.

[65]) Brunner, *Oppositionelle Gruppen*, p.72.

[66]) Störmer, *Adelsgruppen*, pp.136-47; *idem*, *Früher Adel*, pp.222-3; Brunner, *loc.cit.*. See above for the possible connection of Audulf's widow, Keyla, to the Tegernsee founders.

[67]) Borst, "Alkuin", p.56; Fleckenstein, *Hofkapelle* 1, pp.234, 237. For Hildebald's Cologne computistical manuscript see von Euw, "Künstlerische Gestaltung", p.252, and Borst, *Buch der Naturgeschichte*, pp.116-7. Hildebald's association with the "Liber pontificalis" is of note, since, "One of the most obvious characteristics of the *Martyrologium Excarpsatum* [in Book I of the Salzburg *computus* manuscripts] is the number of popes whose names appear in its *laterculi*", and numerous borrowings from the "Liber pontificalis"

II. Political Contexts and Personalities

his influence on the production of the Mondsee *scriptorium*.[68] As Charlemagne's Archchaplain and chief ecclesiastical advisor, he also would have known Audulf well and been closely informed regarding Charlemagne's thoughts and predilections.

The manuscript's route to Regensburg is very uncertain but may lead through a fourth person of some importance in the history of Carolingian Bavaria, Baturich.[69] Baturich first appears in the Regensburg deed evidence as "Paturich archipresbyter" on 21 September 814, shortly after Lothar's despatch to Bavaria, but, from his placement in the witness list, it is not entirely clear whether he was a member of Bishop Adalwin's episcopal *familia* at that date.[70] In the critical year 817, the year of the *Ordinatio imperii* and at the very end of Audulf's tenure, he became Bishop of Regensburg and head of the monastery of St.Emmeram.[71] It is hard to imagine that any high churchman, muchless the Bishop of Regensburg, could have been installed without Audulf's approval or even encouragement, particularly since Regensburg was clearly a prominent center of Audulf's authority. Baturich was a Bavarian who had followed many of his countrymen to the monastery of Fulda where he was a monk and a teacher.[72] He was a scholar of some distinction who was an important collector of manuscripts for Regensburg and was certainly an interested party in the development of Bavaria's status that we have noted above. At Ludwig's accession in 826 he assembled an interesting set of specifically royal, not imperial, ruler-*laudes*, and in 833 he became King Ludwig's Archchaplain.[73]

---

can be demonstrated (McCulloh, "Martyrologium Excarpsatum", p.182).

[68]) Bischoff, *Schreibschulen* II, p.10.

[69]) Note, however, that there is no certainty that Clm 210 was in Regensburg before the late-tenth century (Bishoff, *Schreibschulen* II, p.34).

[70]) Regensburg, *Traditionen*, Nr 13, p.12.

[71]) His first occurrence as Bishop there is in March 819 and a deed of 14 December 819 is dated "tertio [anno] episcopi Baturici" which allows a consecration date as early as late 816 (*Ibid.*, Nrs 15, 16, pp.14-5). The marginal annalistic notes to Clm 210 (46v), the so-called *Annales S.Emmerammi Minores*, place his ordination in the Frankish year 817 which began at Christmas 816 (p.47). The practice of the Regensburg chancery, which dates Louis the Pious' imperial reign from his coronation as Co-Emperor on 11 September 813, seems to differ from that at Freising where the date of his actual succession to Charlemagne at the latter's death on 28 January 814 seems to have been determinative (see the deeds in Freising, *Traditionen*, from Nr 323, pp.277 [18 September 814] onwards still dated to his first regnal year).

[72]) For the Bavarian connections to Fulda see: Störmer, "Adelsgruppe". Hrabanus Maurus, in a poem dedicated to Baturich, calls himself Baturich's "alumnus" ("Versus ad Amicum: Ad Baturicum Episcopum ex Persona Isanberti", Hrabanus Maurus, *Carmina*, p.173). Baturich's connection with Hrabanus may explain the inclusion of the very odd representation of Jove/Jupiter for March discussed above. Recently, Gertrud Diepolder has drawn attention to Baturich's inclusion in the Reichenau memorial book where he occurs in association with an Egilolf and an Otachar ("Freisinger Traditionen", pp.159-64).

In 843, as King Ludwig's representative, Baturich was one of the few East Frankish participants at the West Frankish synod held at Germigny when he would have had ample opportunity to inspect Theodulf's remarkable chapel and to view any mural decorations that may have adorned the adjoining residence.[74] Sometime between 833 and 837, perhaps, even earlier, Mondsee became a proprietary monastery of the Bishopric of Regensburg,[75] and Bischoff has argued that Baturich brought a Mondsee scribe to Regensburg who produced several important manuscripts there.[76]

F. Carolingian Claims and Agilolfing Echoes

One final aspect deserves some attention as we complete our investigation. It can be approached best by recalling the other imperial "works" which Einhard ascribed to Charlemagne in Chapter 29 of his "Life".[77] The first amongst these was an incomplete attempt to reform the laws of his own people, the Franks, and to reduce to writing the laws of the other peoples within his Empire whose laws had not been written down (*iura quae scripta non erant*). Strictly speaking, the Bavarians did not fall into this latter category, since their law-code probably had existed in some unified written form since the middle of the eighth century.[78] Nevertheless, it is a fact that no surviving manuscript of the Bavarian Code predates the early ninth century.[79]

One way to account for this peculiarity is to assume that all older copies of the Code were called in sometime after the Frankish annexation in 788 and that new, revised copies were issued subsequently. Such a process would have permitted the useful additions (*quae deerant addere*) and, more to the point, the correction of those elements which were harmful and defective (*prava quoque ac perperam prolata corrigere*) much as Charlemagne wished to perform for his own people. Certainly, given the zeal with which Charlemagne engineered the downfall of his cousin Tassilo and the termination of his Agilolfing line, we should expect that amongst those things considered most "harmful" and fit for correction would have been any provisions which related to the old political order. Indeed, a paragraph was inserted in three early-ninth-century manuscripts which circulated outside Bavaria in western Francia and northern Italy containing a highly-charged, albeit anonymous reference, to Tassilo's "contempt" for the King's authority and ordaining that

---

[73]) Bischoff, "Bücher", p.187; these *laudes* are discussed above; Fleckenstein, *Hofkapelle* 1, pp.168-170.

[74]) MGH, Concilia, vol.3: "Signum Bathaeum Ragnesburg episcopi [sic]" (p.5).

[75]) Mondsee, *Traditionsbuch*, p.73.

[76]) *Schreibschulen* II, p.11.

[77]) MGH, p.33; Rau, *Quellen*, p.200/1.

[78]) There is a short discussion of several key issues regarding the Bavarian Code in my paper, "*Lex scripta*".

[79]) There is an excellent discussion of the manuscript tradition by Kottje, "Lex Baiuvariorum", esp.the Table on pp.20-1.

such a Duke should not only be deprived of his office but also forfeit any hope of salvation.[80]

It is, therefore, with some surprise that we find in all the early manuscripts that the entire second Chapter or Title of the Code "Concern[s] Dukes and the Matters that Pertain to Them", that is, regulates an office that had not existed since Tassilo's deposition. Even more incongruous is the first paragraph of the third Chapter which sets the wergeld for five noble lineages (i.e. the *genealogiae* including the Huosi) and, in addition, for the Agilolfings, "who are of the ducal line...the supreme rulers amongst you...[and] from whose line the Duke always has been and ought to be, as the Kings, our ancestors granted to them. Whoever from their line was faithful to the King and prudent, him they established as Duke to rule over that people".[81]

This endorsement of the deposed and, presumably, disgraced Agilolfings is, in fact, found in all the major manuscript traditions and occurs in all seven of the extant ninth-century manuscripts, not only the three circulating in Bavaria, but also in both north Italian and west Frankish examplars, indicating an official, royal promulgation.[82] Nor are we dealing here with scholarly imaginings; the oldest Bavarian and other texts were clearly working copies used in daily legal and administrative practice.[83] Therefore, I think we must conclude that the reintroduction of an Agilolfing line into the vacant Bavarian ducal office was both approved and anticipated by Bavaria's

---

[80]) LB II, 8a: "Si quis autem dux de provincia illa quem rex ordinaverit, tam audax aut contumax aut levitate stimulatus seu protervus et elatus vel superbus atque rebellis fuerit, qui decretum regis contempserit: donatum dignitatis ipsius ducati careat, etiam et insuper spem supernae contemplationis sciat se esse condemnatum et vim salutis amittat". These textual variants are most easily followed in the older folio edition by J.Merkel which does not attempt to establish a single, "correct" text (Lex *Baiuwariorum*, p.390, here cited from Merkel's "Textus Legis Tertius", [= Manuscripts E1, E3, E6]).

[81]) "...Agilolvingas...qui sunt de genere ducali...summi principes sunt inter vos...Dux vero...ille semper de genere Agilolvingarum fuit et debet esse, quia sic reges antecessores nostri concesserunt eis; qui de genere illorum fidelis regi erat et prudens, ipsum constituebant ducem ad regendem populum illum" (here cited from Merkel's "Textus Legis Primus", *Lex Baiuwariorum*, p.289). This is the first extant use of the family name, "Agilolfing", as a collective substantive, perhaps, itself a programmatic development (Jarnut, *Agilolfingerstudien*, p.11). The closely-related Alemannic Law Code has no parallel to this passage which is unique in its attention to the exclusive claims of the Agilolfing family, not merely to the office and the person of the Duke.

[82]) See Kottje's Table ("Lex Baiuvariorum", pp.20/1). For Bavaria: Manuscripts B1, A3, B2; for Italy: E1, A4; for Francia: E3, E6.

[83]) Hammer, "*Lex scripta*", p.189. The, apparently, oldest, the Bavarian Codex Ingolstadensis, is in a "pocket book" format, perhaps for use by a Sheriff. Its production may be associated with Bishop Baturich and his collection of royal *laudes* (Bischoff, *Schreibschulen* I, pp.249-50).

Carolingian rulers. And, indeed, there was a precedent near to hand in Bavaria.

To understand this requires an expansion of our view of the Agilolfing family which had existed as the most illustrious of all European aristocratic houses over centuries in numerous lines in Francia, Burgundy, Alemannia, and Langobardic Italy.[84] Their relationship to the Frankish Arnulfings was complex. The Agilolfings provided dangerous opposition to the rise of the Arnulfings as Mayors of the Palace and later Frankish Kings but also conferred on them a heightened aristocratic legitimacy through intermarriage. For their part, the Arnulfings used Agilolfing dynastic claims to advance their own expansionist interests. An example was Carl Martell who provided Frankish support to establish Tassilo's own father, Duke Odilo, the son of the Alemannic Agilolfing Duke, Gottfried, as something of a Frankish "carpetbagger" in Bavaria, thereby terminating the succession of the established Bavarian Agilolfing line with his predecessor, Duke Hugbert.[85]

The opposition to Odilo by powerful factions within the Bavarian aristocracy was so strong that he was driven into exile at the Frankish Court in 740/1 where he apparently seduced and impregnated Carl's daughter and Charlemagne's aunt, Hiltrud, who, amidst dynastic intrigues and against the will of her brothers, Carlomann and Pippin, subsequently became Odilo's wife and Tassilo's mother.[86] This was the scandal of

---

[84]) The scholarship on European-wide connections of the various branches of the Agilolfing family is both confusing and still incomplete. A good starting point for Bavaria is Störmer, *Adelsgruppen*, pp.16-41; and his more recent contribution, "Herzogsgeschlecht", pp.141-52. There are some fascinating "conceptual models" on the very early history of the family developed by J.Jarnut in his *Agilolfingerstudien*. Jarnut adduces an Aquitanian Senator at the head of the family's diffusion, reminiscences of which may close the loop on Agilolfing affinity for Classical seasonal images (*ibid.*, p.125)!

[85]) Odilo's descent, now generally accepted, was first argued effectively by Erich Zöllner in his 1951 article, "Die Herkunft der Agilulfinger". There is, nevertheless, still some question as to whether Gottfried himself was an Agilolfing or whether the descent derived from his anonymous wife (Störmer, *Adelsgruppen*, p.37, and "Herzogsgeschlecht", p.148). See most recently Jahn, *Ducatus Baiuvariorum*, pp.123-8. Friedrich Prinz, following Bernhard Bischoff, has argued that a Carolingian reworking (possibly at the court of Ludwig the German?) of the *Vita* ("Life") of Emmeram, Regensburg's patron saint, relates Emmeram's early 8th-century martyrdom by Lantbert, a son of Duke Theodo of Bavaria, to some final extinction of the Agilolfing line with Tassilo (Prinz, "Arbeo von Freising", p.588; Bischoff, *Leben und Leiden*, pp.95-6). But the passage is worded too narrowly to be construed as a Carolingian witness to the extinction of the Agilolfing family in general. Indeed, I think the more probable interpretation is to understand it as a comment on the failure of Theodo's line with Hugbert in about 736 (Arbeo, *Vita Sancti Haimhrammi*, c.28, p.67: "...ita ut ex omni inmensa infantum procreatione nullus superstes existeret intra paucos quasi annos qui regnum paternum suscipere a Domino mereretur"). For Carl Martell's connubial relationship to the Agilolfings see Schieffer, "Karl Martell", pp.310-14.

II. Political Contexts and Personalities

the century! Outraged echoes of it are still heard in the following century in the anonymous "Astronomer's" biography of Louis the Pious where he remarks as a matter of common knowledge that Louis was concerned that something similar might arise from the love affairs of his sisters, "and, thus, took care lest the outrage recur which once had happened between Odilo and Hiltrud".[87] This enormous stain on the honor of the Arnulfing family must have weighed heavily with Charlemagne and conditioned his attitude towards his unwelcome first cousin, Duke Tassilo, a grudge which issued, as we saw, in the extinction of the latter's line. Indeed, we may get some sense of Charlemagne's resentment when, shortly after Tassilo's subjection in 788, Charlemagne granted the Bavarian monastery of Chiemsee to the episcopal church of Metz, a bishopric with old and intimate connections to the Arnulfing dynasty. In the preamble he notes how, "...from out of the Kingdom of the Franks, the Duchy of Bavaria had been withdrawn and alienated from Us for some time through the infidelity of those evil men, Odilo and Our close kinsman, Tassilo..."[88] The reference to Odilo seems completely gratuitous and can best be understood as a reference to a wrong which finally had been avenged against Tassilo, "Our close kinsman" and the issue of that scandalous liaison.

But the story is even more complex! In the discussion of the "prefects" above, it was pointed out that Gerold (almost certainly) and Audulf (possibly) had Agilolfing dynastic connections. Gerold and his sister, Hildegard, Charlemagne's third wife, both traced their descent through their mother, Imma, the wife of an earlier Gerold, a Frankish magnate on the Middle Rhine. Imma herself was (so Thegan asserted) the great-granddaughter of the same Alemannic Duke, Gottfried, who was Duke Odilo's father and Duke Tassilo's grandfather. With the elimination of Tassilo and his descendants, Imma's children carried the strongest claims to Agilolfing descent, since Carlomann had destroyed the last of the Alemannic Agilolfing Dukes, Theudbald, and annexed Alemannia in 746.[89] Imma's daughter, Hildegard, had several children by Charlemagne, amongst whom was Louis the Pious. Although Hildegard's father, Gerold, was apparently a person of some account, Louis' biographer, Thegan, clearly saw the

---

[86]) Jahn, *Ducatus*, pp.172-8. See, most recently, the comments by Schieffer in "Karolingische Töchter", p.128, and "Karl Martell", p.314.

[87]) "...et cavens ne, quod per Hodilonem et Hiltrudem olim acciderat, revivesceret scandalum..." (Astronomus, *Vita Hludowici imperatoris*, MGH, pp.348/9; Rau, *Quellen*, pp.290/1). I do not believe that the evidence is sufficient to sustain Matthias Becher's ingenious and interesting interpretation of this event as *lèse majesté* in any strict sense ("Zum Geburtsjahr Tassilos", pp.4-6).

---

[88]) "Igitur quia ducatus Baioarie ex regno nostro Francorum aliquibus temporibus infideliter per malignos homines Odilonem et Tassilonem, propinquum nostrum, a nobis substractus et alienatus fuit..." (MGH, Diplomata Karolinorum, vol.1, Nr 162, p.219). Tassilo had a particularly close association with Chiemsee which may account for Charlemagne's action (Diepolder, "Tassilo", p.58).

[89]) See the genealogical diagramm in Störmer, "Das Herzogsgeschlecht", p.151.

Alemannic-Agilolfing connection as the more illustrious descent, surely reflecting the thinking of the Emperor and his son, Ludwig, for whom Thegan exhibits a distinct partisanship.[90] Thus, it appears that Louis and his sons were conscious of their participation in Agilolfing descent., and, accordingly, all of the lay magnates exercising direct power in Bavaria after the deposition of Duke Tassilo, the Prefect Gerold, the Sheriff Audulf, and the Bavarian Kings Lothar and Ludwig, were "Agilolfings"! From this perspective Ludwig's royal "pedagogus", Egilolf, does not seem so strange.

Did any of this matter? Of course, we have only the most indirect of evidence. We may suspect that Gerold, and possibly after him, Audulf, mixed some personal dynastic ambitions into their political designs for Bavaria.[91] This may have been a motive when, shortly before Gerold's surprising and premature death, Salzburg was elevated to the rank of a metropolitan See comprehending in a single entity the whole of the Bavarian polity. However, during the balance Charlemagne's lifetime, in particular, under the terms of the *Divisio Regnorum* of 806, Bavaria seems to have enjoyed no special status. While this situation might still be compatible with the reestablishment of the ducal office under, say, Audulf, after Charlemagne's death things clearly took a much different turn, and the imperial family now asserted their (possibly dynastic) claims on Bavaria directly. With the succession of Louis, Bavaria was invested with full, royal status under the direct rule, successively, of his two sons, Lothar and Ludwig. And Ludwig was ultimately successful in establishing a durable polity, thanks, in large part to his

---

[90]) Thegan, *Vita Hludowici Imperatoris*, MGH, pp.176/7-178/9; Rau, *Quellen*, pp.216/7. Discussion in Jarnut, "Genealogie", p.17. Thegan's tracing Louis' descent through his mother and grandmother contrasts with his account of Charlemagne's, "ancestry back to Arnulf in a strictly agnatic line" (Airlie, "Aristocracy", p.438). For a discussion of Thegan's Carolingian genealogies see also: Tremp, *Studien*, pp.26-8, 91. Thegan's account of the descent through Hildegard is chronologically-possible but not without some problems as was pointed out some time ago but without supporting argumentation by Irmgard Dienemann-Dietrich, "Der fränkische Adel", pp.184-5, but these difficulties were reviewed and resolved in Thegan's favor by Jarnut, "Untersuchungen", pp.23-8. See also the remarks by Donald Bullough in his review article, "*Europae Pater*", pp.78-80. As Bullough implies, the validity of the strictly genetic issue (something further obscured by our deficient knowledge of Duke Gottfried's wife/wives) is rather less important than the descendants' consciousness of it. In this sense, it would be tempting to ascribe the implied claims of this genealogy to Thegan's support for Ludwig the German, since Thegan was writing in the particularly critical years 836/7, but no completely consistent hypothesis suggests itself to me (see Tremp, *Studien*, pp.19-20, 90-1).

[91]) Audulf's line disappeared from prominence in Bavaria with his son, the young Audulf (see above). Yet another Gerold (II), perhaps the nephew or grandson of the Prefect, joined Arn, Audulf and Hildebald as a witness to Charlemagne's testament in 811, was an intimate (and uncle?) of King Ludwig, and served as Prefect of the eastern frontier regions (*Ostland*) until his death in 832 (Brunner, *Oppositionelle Gruppen*, p.82; Wolfram, *Geburt Mitteleuropas*, p.195).

II. Political Contexts and Personalities

Bavarian subjects, "whose loyalty to [him] remained unwavering".[92]

CONCLUDING OBSERVATIONS

This oft-noted fidelity of the Bavarians, that is to say, the Bavarian aristocracy, to Ludwig, was, I think, not fortuitous, but, rather, the result of many years of political preparation. And now it is time to sum up these rather discursive explorations and consider how the two computistical manuscripts, Vienna Codex 387 and Munich Clm 210, and particularly how their novel illustrations of the "labors of the months" might fit into this context, if only as a modest part of a larger effort.

All of the possible pretexts for the creation and every line of transmission for these two Bavarian manuscripts run back through a distinguished layman and three learned clerics of Bavarian descent or relation. All had wide-ranging Frankish connections, and three (Audulf, Arn, Hildebald), were bound together as witnesses to Charlemagne's will and belonged to the highest and most cultivated circles of the Carolingian Court at Aachen, while a fourth, Baturich, was at the very center of Ludwig's East Frankish court. Two of them, Audulf and Arn, played crucial roles in the "reconstruction" of the Bavarian polity after its Frankish annexation. And a fourth Bavarian cleric, Bishop of Hitto of Freising, may also be reckoned to this group because of his clearly close connections to Audulf and his wife, Keyla, and because of his membership in the most important of Bavaria's aristocratic *genealogiae*, the Huosi.

Given this potent context, we must consider whether the "labors of the months" can be associated with any common ideology or any common sentiment which bound together some or all of the potential patrons. Certainly, at one level, like Charlemagne's naming of the Months and the Winds, these pictures are a clear expression of an imperial political ideology. Their purpose would have been to rework an established Classical tradition in an appropriate way to assert the creative power of imperial authority to order human affairs within the context of nature and the cosmos. Through a reordering or rearrangement Classical images (only partially achieved), the "labors" supplemented (but did not replace) the ancient signs of the zodiac with new signs of purposeful human activity responding to the natural procession of the Seasons. At the same time, through the *computus*, their manuscripts served to order sacred time, allowing men to celebrate properly the great feast of the Resurrection, and, thereby, securing Divine Favor for the Empire. This is certainly "political" in the sense advanced above.

In early-ninth-century Bavaria such a political program was, perhaps, especially necessary. It solidified Bavaria's place within the Frankish *imperium* and secured a new and pivotal political role for it in the governance of the emerging East Frankish kingdom. Nor was this accomplished in disregard of Bavaria's Agilolfing political heritage. Rather, this dynastic claim was reestablished on an entirely new and highly successful basis. For Audulf's young protege, Ludwig the German, there would have been the added enticement to enhance himself and, possibly, his capital city, Regensburg, through

---

[92]) See the recent remarks by Johannes Fried in his contribution, "The Frankish Kingdoms", p.144.

identification with the visual artefacts of royal power, a task made more urgent by the skill which his half-brother, Charles, obviously displayed in this regard. Just as the Roman Emperors enlisted the Four Seasons to the cause of imperial power, so also were the Twelve Months pressed into service first, for the Frankish *imperium* and then for the realm of the Bavarians.

Perhaps, too, there was an element of nostalgia at work, as the aging followers of Charlemagne, Arn, Audulf and, perhaps, Hildebald, attempted under a new and somewhat unsympathetic order to preserve the memory of their old lord, carry forward his accomplishments, and recreate something of the fading intellectual and cultural elan that had characterized the Court they had served in their heyday.[93] Possibly, as a final gesture, those aging Bavarian servants of Carolingian rule sought, in the wake of the *Ordinatio imperii* of 817, to cap their efforts by means of a fitting monument, one that would enhance the royal authority of their young beneficiary through a prominent display of learning and art to ensure a right relationship with Heaven and a right order amongst men? The result, however, was mixed, and the "Three-Book" *computus* soon joined the two other notable Carolingian "stillbirths" considered in this essay, the *Libri Carolini* and the renamed months. Today only a single page of both large manuscripts is known and regarded beyond a small group of specialists--but for the wrong reason. Despite their attractive simplicity and apparent realism, the Salzburg "labors of the months" are not faithful contemporary illustrations of rural life in Bavaria or anywhere else in the Carolingian Empire. Rather, they are skillful adaptations of Classical materials and were designed to advance an ideological program of political authority.

---

[93]) This seems to underlie Borst's interpretation: "In den Bücherstuben spiegelte sich, was im Land vorging...Ludwig der Fromme ließ seit 814 nichts vom bohrenden Interesse des Vaters an kosmischer Ordnung des Diesseits erkennen..." (*Buch der Naturgeschichte*, p.170).

Appendix: Wandalbert of Prüm on the Months

WANDALBERTI PRUMIENSIS DE MENSIUM DUODECIM NOMINIBUS SIGNIS CULTURIS AERISQUE QUALITATIBUS

Nominibus mensum quae sit rationis origo,

Annum bis seno volvunt qui sidere magnum,

Quae inlustrent pariter duodenas signa Kalendas,
Quid connexa ferat mensum discretio terris,

Quos usus generet cultus, quos formet habendi:
Servato breviter referemus in ordine, lector.

De Ianuario.

Quem primum mensem servari Iulius anni

Decrevit, Iani effertur cognomine regis,
Saturni gentem Latio qui rexit et urbem
Laurentum sceptris populoque et legibus auxit.
Huic gemino praesunt Capricorni sidera monstro,
Bis duodena uno pariter splendentia signo.

Tum tempus campis lepores lustrare nivosis,

Artibus et variis pictas captare volucres,

Per campos volitant, colles quae et flumina circum.
Tum capus accipiterque placet, curisque solutis
Per brumam genio vacat indulgere, domique

WANDALBERT OF PRÜM ON THE NAMES, THE SIGNS, THE LABORS, AND THE WEATHER CONDITIONS OF THE 12 MONTHS

What is the origin for the names of the months,

Which twice six times turn the great year in season,

Which signs, likewise, illuminate the twelve Calends,
What the successive distinction of the months means for the lands,

What practices cultivation begets, what sort of occupation it regulates:
Reader, we would set forth briefly in the observed order.

Concerning January

Which Julius decreed to be observed as the first month of the year,

It is designated by the name of King Janus
Who ruled the people of Saturn in Latium and
Increased the town of Laurentum in authority and in people and in laws.
Over this twin monstrosity preside the stars of Capricorn
Twice twelve in splendor together in one zodiac sign.

In that season, the hares cavort in the snowy fields,

And by various crafts they trap the painted birds

That fly about the fields, the hills and streams.

Then it pleases, free of cares, to indulge the sparrow-hawk
In its taste for capon throughout the Winter, and at home

Diversos usus veri proferre futuro.	By diverse means to prepare for coming Spring.
Nam neque tum cervos cervasve agitare fugaces	But then is not the time to chase the fleet stags and hinds,
Nec spumantis apri lato configere ferro	Nor is it of use to transfix the shoulder of the foaming boar with iron:
Armos ex usu est: Borea cohibentur et artus	They are restrained by Boreas, and leanness
Exesos macies stringit tenuatque ferarum,	Wastes and shrinks the enfeebled limbs of the beasts.
Semina nec cultis facile est committere terris.	Nor is it easy to commit seed to the tilled land.
Urit cuncta gelu et glacies riget horrida campis;	Everything withers in frost, and a terrible hardness stiffens the fields.
Robora tum silvis prodest et fissile lignum	Then are trees at their strongest, and it is profitable to fell the fissile wood,
Caedere, tum domibus classique aptare secures.	Then to apply axes for dwellings and boats.

De Februario. — Concerning February

Anni quo numerum regnans Pompilius auxit,	While Pompilius reigned he increased the accustomed number of the year,
Quo sacra dira urbem solitum lustrare togatam,	When awful rites were celebrated to purify the City of the Toga,
Inferni Februi retinemus nomine dictum;	Of which we still retain that called by the name of Infernal Februus.
Bis sex hunc stellis astrum praesignat Aquari;	Twice six with stars he marks out the constellation of Aquarius;
Quam tamen australi caelo demittere nimbis	Which, although perceived to set amidst mists in the southern sky,
Cernitur, haec fulget tricenis ignibus unda.	The atmosphere glistens with a thirty-fold glow.
Hunc hiemis verisque tenent confinia mensem,	The boundaries of Winter and Spring comprehend this month,
Frigore nuncque riget, nunc aere mulcet amico.	For now it is stiff with cold, now softened by a friendly breeze.
Tum tempus tractis terram proscindere aratris,	In that season it is good to break up the earth with drawn plows,
Semina et hinc sulcis prodest mandare secundis.	And, thereafter, to entrust seeds to the resulting furrows.
Hordea tum campis serimus peregrina per agros.	Then in the fields we sow the rude barley throughout the plowlands.

Appendix: Wandalbert of Prüm on the Months

Postquam candet avis pietatis nomine praestans,	As soon thereafter as the fair bird appears, vouching in the name of duty,
Vitibus hinc cultum mos est adhibere putandis,	At such time, it is customary to apply oneself to cultivation by the pruning of the vines,
Sarmentisque novas gemmas proferre recisis,	And to bring forth new jewels by cutting off twigs.
Incipiunt salices nodis canescere glaucis	The willows begin to whiten with greyish knobs,
Cum primum et coryli nucibus frondere futuris.	When first also the hazel becomes green with future nuts.
Tunc canibus cervas spiculisque agitare repertas	Then, as hunters, it is pleasant to flush out the hinds and chase them with hounds and sharp-pointed spears,
Ac valido aprorum praefigere corpora ferro,	And to transfix the boars' bodies with stout iron,
Informesque cavis ursos lustrare sub antris	And the hideous bears stirring beneath in the empty caverns;
Venantum de more placet; tunc piscibus altas	Then also to set high fences in the teeming stream as weirs for fishes.
Praestruere aggeribus piscoso in flumine saepes.	

De Martio. — Concerning March

Martius, exortum statuit cui Romulus anni,	March, which Romulus established as the beginning of the year,
Marte tenet ductum bellorum principe nomen,	Takes its name derived from that Mars, the Prince of Wars,
Quem auctorem generis Remo cum fratre Quirinus	Whom Quirinus believed to be the author of his race,
Credidit esse sui, duplicis cui sidera Piscis	Together with his brother Remus, over which the stars of
Praesunt, tricenis senisque micantia flammis.	Double Pisces command, sparkling by sixes in thirty flames.
Hunc mensem iucunda fovent exordia veris,	The delightful beginnings of Spring warmly caress this month,
Qui mare, qui terras specie tranquillat amoena.	Which calms the sea and lands in pleasant manner.
Aestus oceani hoc primum consurgere magnos	At this time we first discern the great swells of the ocean surge,
Navibus et pelagi diffundier aequora pictis	With painted ships parting the surface of the sea,
Cernimus atque novos conscendere flumina pisces.	And new fish ascend the rivers.

Charlemagne's Months and their Bavarian Labors

Garrula per sudum volitans cum stridet hirundo,	The prattling swallow flits about in the bright air with a shrill cry,
Aeriasque grues campis residere satisque	And we discern the airy cranes alight in the fields,
Anseris invisum decedere cernimus agmen.	And the flock of content geese depart unseen.
Saepibus hinc ortos primum munire novandos	From this time, first protect with fences the gardens to be renewed,
Immundoque fimo et rastris componere tempus,	And with foul dung and mattocks arrange the time,
Diversa et propriis committere semina sulcis.	Committing various seeds to their appointed furrows.
Tum cervas, capreas, lepores lustrare voluptas	Then sensuous pleasure causes hinds, she-goats and hares to
Imperat; hinc apibus sedes statione parandae,	Gambol; now the habitations should be set in place for the bees,
Vere suo cum iam stabulis exire reclusis	In that Springtime, when the hives have been laid open to go out,
Invitat stimulans prolis mellisque cupido.	Then desire attracts, stimulating both offspring and honey.
Deque locis steriles primis tum ferre radices	And from their first locations, bear the barren roots of trees,
Arborum et ignotis scrobibus deponere suetum,	And according to custom, place them in fresh trenches,
Plantas quin etiam fecunda ex arbore lectas	Indeed, the bark born from the sprig of another tree,
Arboris alterius natus de germine cortex	Accepts shoots chosen from a fertile tree,
Accipit inque sinu ferro patefactus ad unguem	And in the space laid open by the iron contains it
Continet: hoc laeti surgunt de semine fructus.	Perfectly: from here the happy fruits arise from the graft.

De Aprili. — Concerning April

Quem Veneri sacrum et proprium dixere priores	Which month the ancients declared holy and fitting to
Mensem, hoc quod vigeat demulcens cuncta voluptas,	Venus, because passion flourishes, caressing everything,
Nomine de Graio ductum vocitamus Aprilem,	We call April, derived from the Greek name,
Vel mage quod terras brumali frigore clausas	Or, more likely, that the lands closed by the Winter's cold,

Appendix: Wandalbert of Prüm on the Months

In varios aperit faetus cogitque fovendo,	It opens and compels by warmth into fruitfulness of various kinds,
Romano tantum excellet sermone vocatus.	Just so it exults to be called in the Roman language.
Stellis huic Aries ternis denisque coruscat,	On its behalf, Aries gleams with stars by threes and tens,
Signorum obliquo qui fulget in ordine primus,	Who shines first in the oblique order of the zodiac,
Huic laetos crines iucundaque tempora Phoebus	Phoebus first adorns its pleasant locks and delightful seasons
Floribus ac viridi primum de fronde venustat.	With flowers and verdure from the folliage.
Hoc nam cuncta suos erumpunt germina partus,	For at this time all buds burst forth
Hoc campi silvaeque et prata recentia mense	In this month, the fields and woods and pastures are fresh
Gramine, fronde satis variis vernantque frutectis	In blade, and on the bough it flourishes full with diverse fruits,
Ad pastumque greges mittunt praesepia cunctos.	While the mangers despatch all their flocks to graze.
Tum Philomela suos exercitat impigra cantus,	Then swift Philomela practices her songs,
Arguta et tectis nidum suspendit hirundo,	The piercing swallow hangs its nest from the roof,
Tum sturni, merulae, turdi silvisque volucres	Then starlings, blackbirds, thrushes and all the other birds of the woods
Suetae multisono permulcent aera cantu,	Caress the airs with many-sounding song,
Turtur cum gemitu pariter raucaeque palumbes	The turtle-dove with its deep plaint and equally the hoarse wood-pigeon
Rurali oblectant fessos studio atque labore.	Amuse the weary with their country zeal and labor.
Venandi hoc eadem est Martis quae mense voluptas.	At this time there are the same pleasures of the hunt as in the month of March.
Interea agricolae insistunt frugesque futuras	Meanwhile, the husbandmen apply themselves and hasten
Saepibus aut fossis properant munire cavatis,	To protect future crops by fences and dug ditches,
Prata vel emissis celerant potare fluentis,	Pastures they are quick to water with diversions from the stream,
Vitibus aut vallos addunt furcasque bicornes	To the vines they add trenches and two-pronged supports,
Corticibusque ligant, ventos ut temnere flantes	And bind them to the bark, so that they might defy the blowing winds,
Pendentes facile et possint portare racemos,	And easily bear the hanging grape clusters;

Gratam neu speciem vineta iacentia turpent,	Lying vines defile the pleasing appearance,
Aut validum indigno mutent perdantque saporem.	And degrade what is sound to inferior quality, and destroy the flavor.

De Maio. / Concerning May

Mercurii matrem falso delusa priorum	The deluded age of the ancients erroneously
Aetas quam coluit, Maium cognomine Maia	Named it Maius for the mother of Mercurius, by the name of Maia,
Insignit vel maiorum de nomine patrum	Whom it revered, or from the name of the Major Fathers,
Dicti pars populi, quae dignior urbe togata	That part of the said people which was more worthy of esteem
Extitit. Huic Taurus ter quino sidere fulgens	In the City of the Toga. To this month Taurus, shining thrice in five-fold stars,
Auricomum praefert aestiva lampade Phoebum,	Displays golden-haired Phoebus by a summery torch,
Inflexoque genu scandentis in aethera Tauri	And on bended knee in the ethereal realm of ascending Taurus,
Frontem Maiades septenis ignibus aurant.	The Maiades gild the brow with seven-fold fires.
Hic veris claudens aestivos incipit orbes	This month concludes the Spring and begins the rounds of Summer,
Tellurisque novas fruges mortalibus aegris	Displaying the new crops of the earth to mortal ills,
Ostendens, calathis primus sua pocula miscet,	In wine cups he first mixes his drafts,
Fragaque de modicis praedulcia colligit herbis,	And collects luscious strawberries from modest stalks,
In spicas cum iam viridantia semina surgunt	Already the sprouting seeds surge up in shoots,
Auritosque tegunt lepores lactentia farra.	And the tender spelt conceals the large-eared hares.
Hoc herbis durum prodest mollire lieum	Now it is good to soften the harsh wine with herbs,
Praesumptisque novercarum vitare venena	And by taking drafts from the drainage ditches,
Potibus in variam quos gignunt arva medellam,	Which the fields produce as a manifold remedy, avoid poisons,
Quin et mutato serpentes aere morbos	And, in truth, with the change of air, it is easy at that time, by custom
Tum medica ex usu facile est depellere cura.	To combat deadly serpents by healing care.

Appendix: Wandalbert of Prüm on the Months

Hoc etiam mense autumno quae rite serantur	At this time, also, what is sown by custom in the Autumn month,
Agricolae ductis invertunt terga iuvencis.	The husbandmen, drawing bullocks, turn over.
Hoc, quibus armentis amor est et cultus habendi,	Now, for the cattle there is affection and care for their maintenance,
Faetando pecori lectum de more maritum	For the breeding herd they produce the customary
Emittunt, gentem dominis qui servet equinam.	Wedding bed, to preserve for the lords the equine race.
Hoc quoque delectum castris acieque probare	Now, also to muster the levy in castles and in battle order,
Tyronem vetus instituit doctrina, simulque	The veteran trains the new recruit, and, at the same time,
Turmis et legione hostis premere arma superbi,	In squads and legion to subdue the arms of the haughty enemy,
Seu classem instructam ventis aptare secundis.	Or to fit out the fleet constructed for the favorable winds.
Tumque favis aestu croceis emissa iuventus	Then, in the heat the young bees sent out from the saffron comb,
Aere sub nido ludit, stabulisque relictis	Play in the open air, and having left its hives,
Ignotas quaerunt vagabunda examina sedes.	The wandering swarm, searches for unknown homes.
Alis saepe etiam bellum stimulisque lacessunt	Often they provoke battle, and with their sharp stings,
In pulchramque ruunt animoso pectore mortem.	They rush with bold breast to a glorious death.

De Iunio.   Concerning June

A Iano sextum statuit quem Iulius anni	Which Julius established as the sixth month of the year,
Mensem, Iunonis retinemus nomine dictum,	From January, we keep by the name of Juno,
Aut populus iunior patribus de more secundus	For the younger people, following the custom of the ancients,
Hoc mensi imposuit servato ex ordine nomen.	Applied to this month a name apart from the observed order.
Huic Gemini aequata praesignant lampade Phoebum,	Gemini distinguish this month with equal light for Phoebus,
Sidere ter quino celsus quos signifer aurat.	By thrice five-fold star which the lofty standard-bearer gilds.

Charlemagne's Months and their Bavarian Labors

Solstitio hic reliquos superat longisque diebus	At the solstice this one exceeds by its long days the other months,
Menses, ad summos caeli qui pervenit orbes.	Which reaches to the highest spheres of heaven.
Torrida et hoc aestas segetes fovet, arvaque primum	At this time it is hot and the Summer warms the grainfields,
Fluminis in speciem culmis undare refertis	And first causes the fields to wave with full stalks in the manner of a river;
Efficit, hoc hortos etiam sua cura revisit	At this time also it returns its attention to the gardens,
Atque holerum iam tunc prodest transponere plantas,	And then it is good to transplant the slips of cabbage,
Dum tenerae in fructum possunt adolescere pinguem.	While they are still delicate and are able to grow up into juicy fruit.
Mox violas atque inde rosas et lilia tempus	Soon it is time to pick the violets and then the roses and
Carpere, et in calathis yachinti iungere florem.	The lilies, and to join them in baskets to the flower of the hyacinth.
Hinc mos lactuca caenas componere dulces	From now on it is the custom to gather lettuces for tasty dishes,
Suavibus atque herbis validos relevare sapores.	And with gentle herbs to increase in strength the flavors.
Allia, caepe suis tunc sunt gratissima sucis,	Garlic and onion are then most abundant in their juices.
Tum quoque menta placet, tumque est satureia salubris,	At that time mint also pleases, then is savory wholesome,
Cum necdum validas concrevit sucus in herbas.	When the juice has not yet concentrated into strong-tasting herbs.
Tunc et dulcis aquae salientem quaerere venam	Then also in fasts it pleases to seek out the flowing vein
Ieiunis placet atque haustu vitare calores.	Of sweet water, and by drinking to avoid the heat of Summer.
Hinc etiam cerasa arboribus decerpere tempus;	From now on it is also the time to pluck cherries from the trees;
Puniceis cerasis succedunt cerea pruna,	Plums follow the red cherries,
Moxque piris primis adduntur mitia mala,	And soon mild apples are added to early pears,
Postquam desecto viduantur prata virore,	Thereafter, the meadows are deprived of their cut verdure,
Agricolae et clauso contemnunt frigora foeno.	The husbandmen defy the times of cold with stored hay.

Appendix: Wandalbert of Prüm on the Months

Glandifera hinc florem per silvas induit arbos.

Henceforth, throughout the woods the nut tree puts on the blossom,

Ipsae et vicino vites iam flore tumescunt.

And the neighboring vines already swell in flower.

De Iulio.

Concerning July

Martis origo, sibi quintum quem signat in anno

Starting with March it marks itself out as the fifth in the year,

Quintilemque suos iussit vocitare Quirinus,

And Quirinus commanded his people to call it Quintilis,

Septimus a Iano medium nunc obtinet annum

Seventh from January, July now occupies the middle of the year,

Iulius, a magnoque excellet Caesare dictus,
Solstitio ardentis Cancri cui sidera fulgent

It exults, being named for the Great Caesar,
At the Solstice the four stars of blazing Cancer gleam upon it,

Quattuor et denis pariter radiantia flammis.

And radiate their shine equally in ten-fold flame.

Hunc paribus spatiis centri demissa per axem

Set on the heavenly axis at equal distances about the center,

Consotiat sexto solis lux aurea mensi.

The golden light of the sun unites it with the sixth month.

Faecundae hoc segetes culmis flavescere summis
Incipiunt et spem messis matura referre

At this time, the fertile fields of grain begin to turn to gold on their tallest stalks,
And ripe barley, sown at the first frosts of Autumn,

Hordea sub primis autumni iacta pruinis.
Hoc quoque, quandoquidem iustis fovet ignibus arva
Phoebus, triticeam praebent bona flamina messem.
Hinc etiam lini segetem manus apta requirit:

Conveys the hope of harvest.
Now also, since, Phoebus does, indeed, warm the fields with perfect fires,
The favorable breezes grant the wheat harvest.
From now on, also, the skilled hand seeks out the field of flax:

Nam sata quae fuerit Martis sub mense, refertis
Folliculis reddit maturam Iulius, at quae

For what was sown in the month of March,
July returns with full ears as ripe, and whatever

Per mensem Veneris sulcis est credita raris

Is committed in the month of April to the scattered furrows,

Augusto messem campo dabit ipsa perusto.

That very thing shall bestow the harvest in the burned field of August.

Charlemagne's Months and their Bavarian Labors

Hoc quoque mense piris mensas ornare secundas,	Also, in this month one can adorn the dessert courses with pears,
Praedulcique licet decerpere persica gustu	And pluck the tiny peaches with luscious taste,
Parva, per aestivos primum matura calores	Those which ripen first in the Summer's heat,
Quae existunt, reliqua autumno nam cedere certum est.	The rest it is agreed to yield to Autumn.
Farre etiam primo imbutas libare per aras	Also, from the first spelt, dedicate it upon the early altars,
Tum vacat, ac laetos anni deposcere fructus,	Then cease, and demand the pleasant proceeds of the year,
Cum necdum plenam fundunt sua tempora messem:	Whenever their seasons bring forth the full harvest:
Frugibus et caeli facies oranda sereni est.	For the crops there is the entreating countenance of the bright sky.
Venantum hinc studio pingues agitare repertum	Henceforth, with zeal the huntsmen pursue the fat stags,
Cervos, hinc canibus silvis lustrare sub altis	Now with hounds amongst the high woods,
Corpora, tunc maciem primum vitantia longam,	Their bodies now first escaping their prolonged thinness,
Quam Venus et sterili pepererunt frigora pastu,	Which Venus and the cold by barren fodder begat,
Flore novo certos postquam vineta racemos	In fresh bloom, after the vines produce certain clusters
Gignunt, haec mensem hunc potior nam gratia comit.	For a special favor adorns this month.

De Augusto.   Concerning August

Sextum quem numero et Sextilem Romulus auctor	Which as sixth in number, Romulus the Founder,
Nomine decrevit, Caesar post Iulius anni	Decreed as Sextilis in name, but afterwards Julius Caesar
Censuit octavum, Augusti cognomine Roma	Counted it as the eighth of the year, Rome altering it,
Mutans Octaviano insignem principe dixit.	Marked its name for the ruler Octavian with the added name of Augustus.
Aequali hic spatio Maio cum mense rotatur	This month is turned around in equal interval as is the month of May,
Devexumque tibi moderans, autumne, remittit	And inclined towards your moderation, Autumn, the lamp abates,

Appendix: Wandalbert of Prüm on the Months

Antehac flammigeram volventem lampada solem,	Aforetime, the fiery rolling sun;
Denis octonisque micant cui signa Leonis	For which the signs of Leo sparkle in fires by tens and by eights,
Ignibus, aestivos fundunt quae extrema tepores;	Which at the end pour forth Summer's gentle warmth;
Ac Cererem flavam maturas stringere aristas	And they compel to bind together for golden Ceres the ripe ears,
Cogunt, agricola ad messem cum cingitur omnis	While every husbandman surrounds the harvest,
Cunctaque sudantes producunt arva colonos.	And all the fields bring forth sweating tillers.
Hoc tamen inmensos aether licet aureus ignes	Still, in this month it happens that the golden air
Interdum generet, valido caelumque tremescat	At times produces immense lightnings, shaking the heaven
Murmure et effusi convellant aera nimbi:	With a mighty rumbling, and pouring clouds may rend the skies:
Aestatem autumni componunt tempora laeti.	As the seasons of pleasant Autumn unite with Summer.
Unde viris summo et celeri curanda labore est	Whence, for men, attending to the harvest is the highest and most pressing task,
Messis, et in segetem cuncta exercenda iuventus,	And every youth must be employed in the grainfields,
Maturas imber subitus ne prendere fruges	Lest a violent rainstorm suddenly succeed to snatch away the ripe crops,
Possit et incautum deludat terra laborem.	And the earth mock careless effort.
Nec farris solum stimulat tunc cura metendi	Nor then does zeal for spelt alone set the husbandmen in motion;
Agricolas studium, parilem sed cuncta reposcunt	With the care of reaping, rather, all the fields at once
Arva simul, vario dudum quae semine culta	Demand the same, which only a little while ago were cultivated with different seed,
Post variam tribuunt diverso tempore messem.	Afterwards, they yield in diverse season a various harvest.
Hic linum campus, laetum gerit ille legumen,	This field bears pleasant flax, that one pulse.
Huc invitat avena, vocant huc hordea falcem,	Here oats beckon, there barley summons the sickle,
Nec tenuis vitiae faetus lentisve minutae	Neither the fine fruit of the vine, nor the tiny lentil
Temnitur, inque suos rediguntur singula acervos.	Is scorned, and each is collected into its pile.

Charlemagne's Months and their Bavarian Labors

Hunc quoque per mensem maturos carpere ramis	Also, throughout this month it is proper to pick the ripe fruits of the
Fructus atque epulis fas est superaddere sumptis,	Boughs, and to add them to the already sumptuous repasts,
Ac dulci ficu prunisque pirisque volemis,	And with sweet fig, and plums and warden pears,
Pluribus et nucleis gratos miscere sapores;	And also together with many nuts, to blend the pleasant flavors;
Sacrandosque aris modicos de vite racemos	And to choose a few grape clusters dedicated to the altars,
Sumere et autumni foecundum poscere Bachum,	And to summon Autumn's fertile Bacchus,
Mellita atque epulis gustare absinthia sumptis	And to sample honeyed absinthe at the sumptuous feasts
Dulcibus atque favis latices iuvat addere puros.	And to the sweet honey-combs, it helps to add pure cream.

De Septembri. / Concerning September

Nonum nunc anni censemus in ordine mensem,	Now we account for the ninth month in the order of the year,
Septimus a Marte primo statuente Quirino	Seventh from March, which, as Quirinus first decreed,
Qui fuit, antiquo numerum de nomine priscum	Was, in the ancient appelation, the earliest in order,
Nunc quoque et autumni pluvias cum tempore signans.	Now also signifying the showers of the Autumn together with the date.
Virgo cui denis simul octonisque coruscans	Upon which Virgo, glistening with ten-fold and eight-fold
Stellis, flectentem praefert iam lumina Phoebum.	Stars, displays the lights as Phoebus turns its course.
Hoc mense, Augusto superat qui forte, laborem	In this month the husbandmen complete the toil which, by chance,
Agricolae messis clausis quoque frugibus implent.	Remains from August with the harvest over and the crops taken in.
Hoc quoque vinetis custodes ponere tempus,	This is also the time to place watchmen in the vineyards,
Qui accessu fures valeant prohibere vagantes	Who are able to stop wandering thieves from access
Ac laqueo et nodis vulpes prensare dolosas.	And to lay hold of cunning foxes by snare and net.

Appendix: Wandalbert of Prüm on the Months

Tum funda horrisono et crepitu terrere volucres,	Then, with the fearful slingshot and by noisy rattle to scare
Sollicitat quarum variam vindemia pestem,	The birds, from whom the vintage suffers various plagues;
Praedulces celso redolent dum colle racemi,	As the succulent clusters smell sweet upon the high slope,
Dumque legens carpit maturas vinitor uvas,	And while the vinedresser plucks them, selecting only the ripe grapes,
Donec spumanti sudet vindemia musto	Then the vintage ferments in the frothing must
Ac plenum fundat praelo torquente lieum.	And confirms in the twisting press the mature wine.
Quamvis saepe per imbriferos tepefacta calores	Very often through rainy heat under equally-balanced light,
Luce sub aequanda messuram vinea falcem	The warm vineyard requires the harvest knife,
Quaerat et abiecto nudet sua crura coturno	And the vintner, discarding his shoes, bares his legs,
Vinitor, adgestas pedibus qui conterat uvas.	And crushes the collected grapes with his feet.
Servanda hinc etiam brumae sub frigore poma	Also, from now on the apples are picked to be preserved for the cold of Winter,
Carpere et apricis mos est componere tectis.	And it is the custom to gather them in sunny shelters.
Hinc quoque farra suis prodest committere sulcis	Henceforth, also, it is good to commit the spelt to its furrows
Pinguibus atque arvis fruges mandare futuras.	And to consign to the fertile fields the future crops.
Hinc cervos Venerem pingui fervore petentes	Henceforth, to pierce with sharp points the stags in their gross passion
Per nemora et densas spiculis configere silvas,	Pursing Venus through groves and dense woods,
Cum canibus noto delapsa est aura favore,	With hounds, in the stilled air, by admitted inclination,
Venandi Francos docuit studiosa voluptas.	Eager delight in hunting has instructed the Franks.
Hunc mensem iam tunc Libra moderante ruentem	As this month declines and Libra already moderates,
Aequato spatio iunguntur noxque diesque,	The night and the day are joined in equal space,
Cursibus hincque diem superat nox horrida longis.	And henceforth savage night exceeds the day for a long duration.
Vernali sub sole pari coniuncta recursu,	Under the Spring sun they are joined in equal return,

Charlemagne's Months and their Bavarian Labors

Lux iterum donec tenebris potiora tenere	Then again may light begin to take hold of better spaces than the gloom,
Incipiat spatia et fugientem deprimat umbram.	And drive out the fleeing shadows.

De Octobri. / Concerning October

Anni nunc decimum Octimbrem rotat orbita mensem,	Now the circular sphere turns to the tenth month of the year,
Octavum vetus instituit quem spera vocari.	Which it appointed to be called the Eighth in former times.
Is quoque de numero priscum retinere vocamen	It too is known by its first designation in rank,
Noscitur atque imbres pariter signare frequentes.	And equally to indicate frequent rains.
Libra cui pariles caelo cum fecerit horas,	For it Libra, after it had fashioned equal hours in the heavens,
Umentem volvit breviori tramite Phoebum.	Turned damp Phoebus on a shorter course.
Quattuor extendit retrahens quam brachia flammis	Scorpio stretched out four claws as in flames,
Scorpius ardentem iuxta Herigonenque reliquit.	And, withdrawing them, yielded in face of fiery Erigone.
Hunc mensem plenis supplet vindemia labris,	The vintage supplies this month with full vats,
Omnibus atque arvis, mitis quae pampinus ornat,	And, in every field that the ripe tendril adorns,
Undique conductis fervent vineta colonis.	On all sides the vineyards swarm with the assembled tillers.
Hi ferro mites caedunt de palmite fructus,	Some with iron cut the ripe fruits from the vine,
Congestos humeris hi gaudent ferre racemos,	While others rejoice to carry off the gathered clusters of the earth,
Longius hi ductis exportant vitea plaustris	Some bear far away the gifts of the grape in drawn carts,
Munera, at hi validis praelum torquere lacertis	And yet others press on with strong arms by twisting to turn
Instant ac dulci distendunt robora musto;	The contest, and they swell the oaks with sweet must;
Hi quoque vel veteres instaurant undique cupas,	These also renew on every side the old casks,
Sufficiuntve novas solido de robore, cunctum	Or furnish enough new ones from stout oak, that the
Provida quis anni claudant cellaria vinum.	Alloted cellars may hold all the wine from each vintage.

Appendix: Wandalbert of Prüm on the Months

Idem amor accendit cunctos, eademque per omnes	The same passion inflames them all and the same concern
It cura et requiem fessis vix ipsa referre	Amongst them all, and the night is scarcely able
Nox valet exercetque omnes labor unus habendi.	To restore rest to the weary, and a single effort to achieve employs them all.
Tunc etiam lento mustum congesta vapore	Then also the concentrated blaze heats the must in lingering warmth,
Flamma coquit spumasque undanti effundit aeno.	And pours out froth in waving bronze.
Claraque praedulcem servant sic vina saporem	And, thus, the bright wines preserve the pleasing flavor
Ieiunis demum facilem praebentque medelam.	And, indeed, offer quick remedy for those fasting.
Tunc quoque contritum mola vertente synapi	Then also it is good to mix up mustard ground by the turning millstone
Prodest uvarum primo miscere liquori,	With the first juice of the grapes,
Hinc epulas grati relevent ut deinde sapores.	That, thereafter, these pleasant things might increase the sumptuous flavors.
Hoc et mense sues lucis inducere tempus,	And in this month, it is the time to lead the swine into the woods,
Maturo hibernum frangant ut tempore glandem.	That they might grind upon the Autumn nut in proper season.

De Novembri. / Concerning November

Undecimus magno nunc volvitur orbe November,	November, the Eleventh, now revolves upon the great sphere,
Anno quem nonum antiquo dixere parentes,	Which the ancestors called the Ninth in the old year,
Ex numero atque imbri primum nomenque retentat.	From which number and for its heavy rain it keeps the first name.
Scorpius huic denis pariter micat atque novenis	Scorpio shines upon it equally with ten- and nine-fold
Stellis, sed flammae nunc Libram quattuor implent.	Stars, but four flames now fill up Libra,
Astrorum cultrix Chelas quas repperit aetas,	She who tends the stars, which that age perceived as the Chelae, the four arms of Scorpio,
Ter quinoque ardet nunc tantum Scorpius igne.	Thrice only Scorpio now warms with five-fold fire.

Charlemagne's Months and their Bavarian Labors

Hoc mense autumnus hiemi decedere durae	In this month, Autumn begins to withdraw before hard Winter,
Incipit et gelidis conflantur frigora ventis,	And the cold is stirred up by the icy winds,
Aere sed dubio diversam terra figuram	Yet, in the changing climate the earth takes on various shape,
Concipit, in pluvias Zephiro nunc flante soluta,	Now dissolved in showers while Zephyr blows,
Nunc Borea in rigidam speciem concreta furente.	Now stiffened into hard form while Boreas rages.
Hinc, cum forte datis licet exercere sub auris	From now on, when, by chance, under the gift of golden skies it is possible to work the earth,
Terram, proscissis committere semina campis	It is good to commit to the plowed fields those seeds
Prodest, autumno superant quae forte peracto,	Which may remain in excess from the Autumn harvest just completed,
Porcorumque greges silvis consuescere faetis,	And to join the herds of pigs to the fertile woods,
Dum pinguem vento tribuit quassante ruinam	While the oak sheds its rich deposit in the shaking wind,
Quercus dumque nemus glandis vestitur honore.	And while the grove is adorned in dignity with acorns and other nuts.
Tunc et apros silvis cura est quam maxima duros	Then also is greatest attention given to seeking out the hardy boars
Quaerere et ex luco canibus producere nigro,	In the woods and to drive them out of the dark grove with dogs
Dum validos crebris praedurant ictibus armos,	While they toughen their mighty shoulders with repeated blows,
Antiquaque fricant solidandas arbore costas	And rub their firm ribs against the ancient tree,
Caeci nec lato metuunt venabula ferro.	Nor, blinded, do they fear the hunting spears with broad iron.
Quod superest curas genialis bruma resolvens,	For the rest, genial Winter loosening from cares,
Dulcibus ad requiem illecebris vocat, horrida postquam	Summons with sweet charms to rest, after the terrible
Ruralem cohibent ventorum flabra laborem.	Blasts of the winds put a stop to country work.
Tum dulces ludi tumque est gratissimus ignis,	Then playful diversions are agreeable and then the fire most pleasant,
Atque novo oblectat somnum invitare lieo.	And, with new wine, it is comforting to summon sleep.

Appendix: Wandalbert of Prüm on the Months

De Decembri.	**Concerning December**
Extremum bis sena regit nunc linea mensem,	Twice six in line now marks out the final month,
Quem decimum auctore scripsit nova Roma Quirino,	Which young Rome described as the Tenth on the authority of Quirinus,
Nomine qui numerum et nimbos designat eodem,	Who designates the number and by the same name the violent rains,
Nunc etiam Martis dictus de mense December,	Now also called December from the month of March,
Arcitenens Phoebum angustis cui cursibus effert	The Bow-Bearer, transports Phoebus on its narrow courses,
Ternis ac denis praefulgens ignibus una.	Shining at one time with three- and ten-fold flames.
Hoc mense australem caeli demissus in axem	In this month the sun, sunk down to the southern axis of the sky,
Exiguoque orbem perlustrans tramite nostrum	Traversing our vault by a short path
Sol iterum ad Boream convertit lumina celsum.	Once again turns its lights towards lofty Boreas.
Hoc etiam hiberno terras urente rigore	Also, whithering the lands in wintery numbness,
Maxima nox modicae causantes munera lucis	The longest night encourages the husbandmen, pleading for
Agricolas fovet, oblitos tandemque laboris	The employments of moderate light, and, at length, forgetful of their labors,
Ingratosque sibi blandus sopor inrigat artus.	Pleasant sleep refreshes for them the ungrateful limbs.
Nec tamen imbrifero desunt sua munera mensi,	Nevertheless, their duties are not absent in this rainy month,
Nec gelidis cogit penitus cessare sub auris	Nor does the season force to be idle under frosty skies,
Tempus et in faciem tellus contecta nivosam.	Or when the ground is covered with a snowy countenance.
Tum quoque cum pluviis campus ventoque madescit,	At that time, also, when the field is soaked by rain and wind,
Vomere gleba iacens sulcanda est, hordea demum	The lying soil should be broken in furrows by the plowshare,
Qua serere aut laetum cupit exercere legumen	Just then the husbandman desires to sow the barley and to set to work on the willing pulse,
Agricola, inmundumque fimum iactare per agros	And then it is time to spread the foul manure.

Charlemagne's Months and their Bavarian Labors

Tum licet. At cum terra hebeti torpore rigescit,
Multa domi tamen et tectis properare sub ipsis

Mox vacat, algentis relevant quae frigora brumae
Retibus hinc varias pelagi prensare volucres,

Aut igni et sonitu per campos fallere, sive

Lentandis usu pedicas aptare repertum;

Amnibus hinc etiam piscosis ponere crates

Vimineas, densosque ad litora figere fasces,

Qua vada demisso tranquillant flumine cursum,
Inventum, facilem capiant ut retia praedam.

Hoc sub mense sues pasta iam glande madentes,
Distento et plenam monstrantes ventre saginam,
Caedere et ad tepidum mos est suspendere fumum
Terga, prius salis fuerint cum sparsa madore.

Bis sena hos cultus renovant vertigine menses
Huncque modum et morem sibi Gallica rura retentant:
Quem breviter signans digessi carmine, lector,
Wandalbertus ego, hortatu compulsus amici,
Dulcia me Hreni quo tempore litora alebant,

Maxima Agrippinae veteris quis moenia praesunt.

MENSIUM XII DESCRIPTIO EXPLICIT FELICITER AMEN

And when the land stiffens in dull torpor,

Nevertheless, many things at home advance quickly under those very roofs,

And there is scarcely time for leisure, which things mitigate the chills of cold Winter,

From this time to catch various waterfowl with nets,

To deceive with flame and noise through the fields,

Or, having devised by bending for use, to set up snares;

Also now to place hurdles woven out of branches in the swift streams

Full of fish, and to affix thick faggots to the banks,

Which shoals still the course in the lowered river,

Once contrived, as in nets they may capture the easy prey.

In this month, slaughter the pigs filling themselves on the fodder of nuts,

Fully stuffed in appearance and with swollen belly,

And, it is the practice to hang them in warm smoke

After the backs have first been sprinkled with salt water.

Twice six months renew in their round these labors,

And the Gallic countryside holds fast to this practice and custom.

Which, Reader, I, Wandalbert, compelled by the urgings of a friend,

Briefly indicating, have divided up in song,

As the sweet shores of the Rhine were nourishing me in that time,

Where the great walls of Cologne Agrippina preside of old.

HERE THE DESCRIPTION OF THE 12 MONTHS ENDS AUSPICIOUSLY, AMEN.

BIBLIOGRAPHY

Abbreviation:

MGH: Monumenta Germaniae Historica

A. Primary Sources Cited:

Admonitio Generalis, ed.A.Boretius, MGH, Capitularia, vol.1, Nr 22, pp.52-62.

Alcuin, *Carmina*, ed. E.Dümmler, MGH, Poetae, vol.1, pp.160-351.

Alcuin, *Epistolae*, ed.E.Dümmler, MGH, Epistolae, vol.4, pp.1-481.

Angilbert, *Carmina*, ed. E.Dümmler, MGH, Poetae, vol.1, pp.355-81.

Annales Regni Francorum, ed.F.Kurze, MGH, Scriptores Rerum Germanicarum in Usum Scholarum, (Hannover, 1895).

Annales S. Emmerammi Minores, ed.G.Waitz, MGH, Scriptores, vol.13 (Hannover, 1881), pp.47-8.

Annales S.Emmerammi Ratisponensis Maiores, ed.G.H.Pertz, MGH, Scriptores, vol.1, (Hannover, 1826), pp.91-3.

Arbeo, *Vitae Sanctorum Haimhrammi et Corbiniani*, ed.B.Krusch, MGH, Scriptores Rerum Germanicarum in Usum Scholarum, vol.11 (Hannover, 1920).

Astronomus, *Vita Hludowici imperatoris*, ed. and transl. by E.Tremp, MGH, Scriptores Rerum Germanicarum in Usum Scholarum Separatim Editi, vol.64 (Hannover, 1995).

Ausonius, *Eclogae*, ed.and transl.H.G.E.White, Loeb Classical Library, vol.1 of 2 (London & Cambridge, Mass., 1961).

Bede, *De Natura Rerum Liber*, ed.C.W.Jones, in *Bedae Opera*, Pars I (Opera Didascalica 1), Corpus Christianorum, Series Latina, vol.123A (Turnholt, 1975), pp.173-234.

Bede, *De Temporum Ratione Liber*, ed.C.W.Jones, in *Bedae Opera*, Pars VI (Opera Didascalica 2), Corpus Christianorum, Series Latina, vol.123B (Turnholt, 1977), pp.329-32.

Bischoff, B., *Leben und Leiden des Hl.Emmeram. Lateinisch-deutsch* (Munich, 1953).

Breviarius Urolfi, ed.H.Tiefenbach, "Die Namen des Breviarius Urolfi mit einer Textedition und zwei Karten", in *Ortsname und Urkunde. Frühmittelalterliche Ortsnamenüberlieferung*, ed.R.Schützeichel, Beiträge zur Namenforschung, N.F., Suppl.29 (Heidelberg, 1990), pp.60-96.

Capitulare de Villis, ed.A.Boretius, MGH, Capitularia, vol.1, Nr 32, pp.82-91; ed.C.Brühl, Dokumente zur deutschen Geschichte in Faksimiles, Reihe 1, vol.1 (Stuttgart, 1971).

Carmina Salisburgensia, ed.E.Dümmler, MGH, Poetae, vol.2, pp.637-48.

Columella, Lucius Junius Moderatus, *On Agriculture and Trees*, ed.and transl.E.S.Forster and E.H.Heffner, 3 vols., Loeb Classical Library (London & Cambridge, Mass., 1955).

Davis-Weyer, C., *Early Medieval Art 300-1150*, Medieval Academy Reprints for Teaching, vol.17 (Toronto, 1986).

Einhard, *Epistolae*, ed.E.Dümmler, MGH, Epistolae, vol.5, pp.105-49.

Einhard, *Vita Karoli Magni*, ed.G.H.Pertz, G.Waitz and O.Holder-Egger, MGH, Scriptores Rerum Germanicarum in Usum Scholarum, 6th edn (Hannover & Leipzig, 1911; reprint: 1947)

Freising: *Die Traditionen des Hochstifts Freising*, ed. T.Bitterauf, , Pt.1, Quellen und Erörterungen zur bayerischen und deutschen Geschichte, Neue Folge, vol.4 (Munich, 1905; reprint: Aalen, 1967).

Fulda: *Urkundenbuch des Klosters Fulda*, vol.1, ed.E.E.Stengel, Veröffentlichungen der Historischen Kommission für Hessen und Waldeck, vol.10/1 (Marburg, 1958).

Godman, P., *Poetry of the Carolingian Renaissance* (London, 1985).

Hrabanus Maurus, *Carmina*, ed.E.Dümmler, MGH, Poetae, vol.2, pp.154-258.

Hrabanus Maurus, *De Universo Libri XXII*, Migne, PL, vol.111 (Paris, 1852), Cols 9-614.

Liber Pontificalis: *Le Liber Pontificalis; Texte, Introduction et Commentaire*, ed.L'Abbé Duchesne, Bibliothèque des écoles françaises d'Athènes et de Rome, vol.2 (Paris, 1955; reprint: 1981); Engl.transl. with commentary by R.Davis, *The Lives of the Eighth-Century Popes*, Translated Texts for Historians, vol.13, (Liverpool, 1992).

Lex Baiuwariorum, ed.J.Merkel, MGH, Leges, vol.3 (Hannover, 1863; reprint: Leipzig, 1925).

Lex Salica, ed.K.A.Eckhardt, MGH, Leges Nationum Germanicarum, vol.4, pt.2 (Hannover, 1969).

Libri Carolini, ed.H.Bastgen, MGH, Concilia, vol.II, Supplementum, (Hannover & Leipzig, 1924).

Lorsch: *Codex Laureshamensis*, vols.2/3, ed.K.Glöckner (Darmstadt, 1933/1936).

Menologium Rusticum Colotianum/Vallense, Corpus Inscriptionum Latinarum, vol.6,1 (Inscriptiones Urbis Romae Latinae), (Berlin, 1876), pp.637-9.

MGH, Capitularia Regum Francorum, vol.1, ed.A.Boretius (Hannover, 1883).

MGH, Concilia, vol.3 (Die Konzilien der Karolingischen Teilreiche 843-859), ed.W.Hartmann, (Hannover, 1984), pp.1-7 (1.Germigny).

MGH, Diplomata Karolinorum, vol.1, ed.E.Muehlbacher, 2nd edn.(Berlin, 1956).

MGH, Diplomata Regum Germaniae ex Stirpe Karolinorum, vol.1, ed.P.Kehr (Berlin, 1932).

MGH, Epistolae, vol.4 (Epistolae Karolini Aevi, vol.2), E.Dümmler, (Berlin, 1895); vol.5 (Epistolae Karolinie Aevi, vol.3), ed.E.Dümmler (Berlin, 1899).

MGH, Necrologia Germaniae, vol.2, ed.S.Herzberg-Fränkel (Berlin, 1890), pp.91-198 (*Necrologia S.Rudberti Salisburgensis*).

MGH, Poetae, vol.1 (Poetae Latini Aevi Carolini), ed.E.Dümmler (Berlin, 1880/1); vol.2 (Poetae Latini Aevi Carolini), ed.E.Dümmler (Berlin, 1884).

Miniature sacre e profane dell'anno 1023 illustranti l'enciclopedia medioevale di Rabano Mauro, ed.A.M.Amelli, Documenti per la Storia della Miniatura e dell'Iconographia (Montecassino, 1896).

Mondsee: *Das älteste Traditionsbuch des Klosters Mondsee*, ed.G.Rath & E.Reiter, Forschungen zur Geschichte Oberösterreichs, vol.16 (Linz, 1989).

Palladius, Rutilius Taurus Aemilianus, *Opus Agriculturae, De Veterinaria Medcina, De Insitione*, ed.R.H.Rodgers, Bibliotheca Scriptorum Graecorum et Romanorum Teubneriana (Berlin, 1975).

Paul the Deacon, *Historia Langobardorum*, ed.L.Bethmann and G.Waitz, MGH, Scriptores Rerum Langobardicarum et Italicarum Saec.VI-IX (Hannover, 1878; reprint: 1964), pp.12-187; *History of the Lombards*, Engl.transl.W.D.Foulke (Philadelphia, reprint 1974).

Rau, R., *Quellen zur Karolingischen Reichsgeschichte*, Pt.1, Ausgewählte Quellen zur deutschen Geschichte des Mittelalters, vol.5 (Darmstadt, 1955).

Regensburg: *Die Traditionen des Hochstifts Regensburg und des Klosters S. Emmeram*, ed. J.Widemann, Quellen und Erörterungen zur bayerischen und deutschen Geschichte, Neue Folge, vol.8 (Munich, 1943; reprint: Aalen, 1988).

Regino of Prüm, *Chronicon*, ed.F.Kurze, MGH, Scriptores Rerum Germanicarum in Usum Scholarum, vol.28 (Hannover, 1890).

Schlosser, J.von, *Schriftquellen zur Geschichte der karolingischen Kunst*, Quellenschriften für Kunstgeschichte und Kunsttechnik des Mittelalters und der Neuzeit, Neue Folge, vol.4 (Vienna, 1892).

Thegan, *Vita Hludowici Imperatoris*, ed. and transl. by E.Tremp, MGH, Scriptores Rerum Germanicarum in Usum Scholarum Separatim Editi, vol.64 (Hannover, 1995).

Theodulf, *Carmina*, ed.E.Dümmler, MGH, Poetae, vol.I, pp.437-581.

Utrecht Psalter, *Vollständige Faksimileausgabe im Originalformat der Handschrift 32, Utrecht-Pslater, aus dem Besitz der Bibliotheek der Rijksuniversiteit te Utrecht, Codices Selecti*, vol.75, 2 pts, (Graz, 1982/4).

Varro, Marcus Terentius, *On Agriculture*, ed. and transl.W.D.Hooper and H.B.Ash, Loeb Classical Library (London & Cambridge, Mass., 1967).

Virgil, *Eclogues*, ed.and transl.H.R.Fairclough, Loeb Classical Library, vol.1 of 2 (London & New York, 1926).

Wandalbert of Prüm, *Carmina*, ed.E.Dümmler, MGH, Poetae, vol.2, pp.567-622 (of which: "De Mensium Duodecim Nominibus Signis Culturis Aerisque Qualitatibus", pp.604-16; see below, Appendix, for Latin text and English translation).

B. Secondary Sources Cited:

Abel, W., "Landwirtschaft 500-900", in *Handbuch der deutschen Wirtschafts- und Sozialgeschichte*, ed.H.Aubin and W.Zorn, vol.1 (Stuttgart, 1971), pp.83-108.

Airlie, S., "The aristocracy", in *The New Cambridge Medieval History*, vol.2, pp.431-450.

Alföldy, G., *Noricum*, The Provinces of the Roman Empire (London, 1974).

Andrieu, M., *Les 'Ordines Romani' du haut Moyen Age*, vol.1 (Les Manuscrits), Spicilegium Sacrum Lovaniense, Fasc.11 (Louvain, 1931).

Baczko, B., "Le Calendrier Républicain", in *Les Lieux de Mémoire*, ed.P.Nora, vol.1 (La République), (Paris, 1984), pp.37-83.

Die Bajuwaren. Von Severin bis Tassilo 488-788, ed.H.Dannheimer and Heinz Dopsch (Munich and Salzburg, 1988).

Bauerreiss, R., *Kirchengeschichte Bayerns*, vol.1, 2nd edn. (St.Ottilien, 1958).

Becher, M., *Eid und Herrschaft. Untersuchungen zum Herrscherethos Karls des Großen*, Vorträge und Forschungen, Sonderband 39 (Sigmaringen, 1993).

Becher, M., "Zum Geburtsjahr Tassilos III.", *Zeitschrift für bayerische Landesgeschichte*, vol.52 (1989), pp.3-12.

Betz, W., "Karl der Große und die lingua theodisca", in *Karl der Große*, vol.2, pp.300-6.

Bischoff, B. "Bücher am Hofe Ludwigs des Deutschen und die Privatbibliothek des Kanzlers Grimalt", in *idem, Mittelalterliche Studien. Ausgewählte Aufsätze zur Schriftkunde und Literaturgeschichte*, vol.3 (Stuttgart, 1981), pp.187-212.

Bischoff, B., "Libraries and Schools in the Carolingian Revival of Learning", in *idem, Manuscripts and Libraries in the Age of Charlemagne*, ed.and transl.M.Gorman (Cambridge, 1994), pp.93-114.

Bischoff, B., *Die Südostdeutschen Schreibschulen und Bibliotheken der Karolingerzeit*, Part I (Die bayerische Diözesen), 3rd edn. (Wiesbaden, 1974); Pt.II (Die vorwiegend österreichischen Diözesen), (Wiesbaden, 1980).

Bloch, P., "Das Apsismosaik von Germigny-des-Pres, Karl der Grosse und der alte Bund", in *Karl der Große*, vol.3, pp.234-61.

Borst, A., "Alkuin und die Enzykopädie von 809", in *Science in Western and Eastern Civilizaton*, pp.53-75.

Borst, A., *Das Buch der Naturgeschichte. Plinius und seine Leser im Zeitalter des Pergaments*, Abhandlungen der Heidelberger Akademie der Wissenschaften, Phil.-hist.Kl., 1994/1 (Heidelberg, 1994).

Borst, A., "Computus-Zeit und Zahl im Mittelalter, *Deutsches Archiv für Erforschung des Mittelalters*, vol.44 (1988), pp.1-82.

Borst, A., *The Ordering of Time; From the Ancient Computus to the Modern Computer*, Engl.transl.(Cambridge, 1993).

Bosl, K., *Franken um 800. Strukturanalyse einer fränkischen Königsprovinz*, 2nd edn. (Munich, 1969).

Bowlus, C., *Franks, Moravians and Magyars; The struggle for the Middle Danube, 788-907*, (Philadelphia, 1995).

Brühl, C., *Fodrum, Gistum, Servitium Regis. Studien zu den wirtschaftlichen Grundlagen des Königtums im Frankenreich...*, Pt.1, Kölner Historische Abhandlungen, vol.14 (Cologne, 1968).

Brunner, K., "Fränkische Fürstentitel. III,2.Bayern", in *Intitulatio II. Lateinische Herrscher- und Fürstentitel im 9. und 10.Jahrhundert*, ed.H.Wolfram, Mitteilungen des Instituts für österreichische Geschichtsforschung, Ergänzungsband 24 (Vienna, 1973), pp.235-46.

Brunner, K., *Oppositionelle Gruppen im Karolingerreich*, Veröffentlichungen des Instituts für österreichische Geschichtsforschung, vol.25 (Vienna, 1979).

Bullough, D., "*Europae Pater*: Charlemagne and his Achievement in the Light of Recent Scholarship", *English Historical Review*, vol.85 (1970), pp.59-105.

Bullough, D., *The Age of Charlemagne*, 2nd edn. (London, 1973).

Butzer, K.W., "The Classical Tradition of Agronomic Science: Perspectives on Carolingian Agriculture and Agronomy", in *Science in Western and Eastern Civilization*, pp.539-96.

Cambridge: *The New Cambridge Medieval History*, vol.2 (*c*.700-*c*.900), ed.R.McKitterick (Cambridge, 1995).

Clausen, W., *A Commentary on Virgil 'Eclogues'* (Oxford, 1994).

Comet, G., "Les calendriers médiévaux, une représentation du monde", *Journal des Savants*, 1992, pp.35-98.

Czysz, W., et.al., *Die Römer in Bayern* (Stuttgart, 1995).

Dienemann-Dietrich, I., "Der fränkische Adel in Alemannien im 8. Jahrhundert", in *Grundfragen der Alemannischen Geschichte*, ed.T. Mayer, Vorträge und Forschungen, vol.1 (Lindau/Constance, 1954; reprint: 1962), pp.149-92.

Diepolder, G., "Freisinger Traditionen und Memorialeinträge im Salzburger *Liber Vitae* und im Reichenauer Verbrüderungsbuch. Auswertung der Parallelüberlieferung aus der Zeit der Bischöfe Hitto und Erchanbert von Freising", *Zeitschrift für bayerische Landesgeschichte*, vol.58 (1995), pp.147-89.

Diepolder, G., "Tassilo, Herzog der Bayern", in *Lebensbilder aus der Geschichte des Bistums Regensburg*, Part 1, ed.G.Schwaiger, Beiträge zur Geschichte des Bistums Regensburg, vols.23/24 (Regensburg, 1989), pp.53-80.

Dodwell, C., *Painting in Europe, 800-1200* (London, 1971).

Dufrenne, S., *Les illustrations du psautier d'Utrecht. Sources et apport carolingien*, Association des publications près les universités de Strasbourg, fasc.161 (Paris, 1978).

Eastwood, B., "Plinian astronomical diagrams in the early Middle Ages", in *Mathematics and its applications to science and natural philosophy in the Middle Ages; Essays in honor of Marshall Clagett*, ed.E.Grant and J.E.Murdoch (Cambridge, 1987), pp.141-72.

Eastwood, B., "The Astronomies of Pliny, Martianus Capella and Isidore of Sevilla in the Carolingian World", in *Science in Western and Eastern Civilizaton*, pp.161-80.

Elias, N., *Time: An Essay*, Engl.transl. (Oxford, 1992).

Bibliography

Englisch, B., *Die Artes Liberales im frühen Mittelalter (5.-9.Jh.)*, Sudhoffs Archiv, Beiheft 33 (Stuttgart, 1994).

Eschweiler, J., et.al., *Der Stuttgarter Bilderpsalter. Bibl.Fol.23 Württembergische Landesbibliothek Stuttgart*, vol.2 (Untersuchungen) (Stuttgart, 1968).

Euw, A.von, "Die künstlerische Gestaltung der astronomischen und komputistischen Handschriften des Westens", in *Science in Western and Eastern Civilizaton*, pp.250-69 + Plates.

Finck von Finckenstein, A.Graf, "Fest- und Feiertage im Frankenreich der Karolinger", in *Beiträge zur Geschichte des Regnum Francorum. Referate beim Wissenschaftlichen Colloquium zum 75. Geburtstag von Eugen Ewig am 28. Mai 1988*, ed.R.Schieffer, Beihefte der Francia, vol.22 (Sigmaringen, 1990), pp.121-9.

Fleckenstein, J., "Alcuin im Kreis der Hofgelehrten Karls des Großen", in *Science in Western and Eastern Civilization*, pp.3-21.

Fleckenstein, J., "Karl der Große und sein Hof", *Karl der Große*, vol.I, pp.24-50.

Fleckenstein, J., "Missus/missaticum", in *Lexikon des Mittelalters*, vol.6 (Munich/Zurich, 1993), cols.679-80.

Fleckenstein, J., *Die Hofkapelle der deutschen Könige*, Pt.1 (Grundlegung. Die Karolingische Hofkapelle), Schriften der MGH, vol.16,1 (Stuttgart, 1959).

Folz, R., *The Coronation of Charlemagne, 25 December 800*, Engl.transl.(London, 1974).

Freeman, A., "Carolingian Orthodoxy and the Fate of the Libri Carolini", *Viator*, vol.16 (1985), pp.65-108.

Freeman, A., "Scripture and Images in the Libri Carolini", in *Testo e immagine*, pp.163-95.

Fried, J., "The Frankish Kingdoms, 817-911: The East and Middle Kingdoms", in *The New Cambridge Medieval History*, vol.2, pp.142-68.

Fried, J., *Der Weg in die Geschichte. Die Ursprünge Deutschlands bis 1024*, Propyläen Geschichte Deutschlands, vol.1 (Berlin, 1994).

Friese, A., *Studien zur Herrschaftsgeschichte des fränkischen Adels. Der mainlädisch-thüringische Raum vom 7. bis 11.Jahrhundert*, Geschichte und Gesellschaft: Bochumer Historische Studien, vol.18 (Berlin, 1979).

Fussell, G., *The Classical Tradition in West European Farming*, (London,1972).

Ganshof, F.L., *Frankish Institutions under Charlemagne*, Engl.transl.(New York, 1968).

Gaulin, J.-L., "Tradition et pratiques de la littérature agronomique pendant le haut moyen age", in *L'ambiente vegetale nell'alto medioevo*, Settimane di studio, vol.37,1 (Spoleto, 1990), pp.103-35.

"The Gentle Voices of Teachers"; Aspects of Learning in the Carolingian Age, ed.R.Sullivan (Columbus, 1995).

Geschichte Salzburgs. Stadt und Land, vol.1 (3 parts), ed.H.Dopsch (Salzburg, 1981-4).

Geuenich, D., "Die volkssprachige Überlieferung der Karolingerzeit aus der Sicht des Historikers", *Deutsches Archiv für Erforschung des Mittelalters*, vol.39 (1983), pp.104-30.

Gockel, M., *Karolingische Königshöfe am Mittelrhein*, Veröffentlichungen des Max-Planck-Instituts für Geschichte, vol.31 (Göttingen, 1970).

Godman, P., *Poets and Emperors; Frankish Politics and Carolingian Poetry* (Oxford, 1987).

Goldberg, E.J., "'Dilectissimus Pater Aquila Transalpinus'; Archbishop Arn of Salzburg and Charlemagne's 802 Administrative Reforms", University of Virginia M.A.Thesis (1994).

Hamann, S., "Frühe genealogische Verbindungen um das Patrozinium St. Lambert", in *Regensburg, Bayern und Europa: Festschrift* für Kurt Reindel zum 70. Geburtstag, ed. L.Kolmer and P.Segl (Regensburg, 1995), pp.49-69.

Hammer, C., "Country Churches, Clerical Inventories and the Carolingian Renaissance in Bavaria", *Church History*, vol.49 (1980), pp.5-17.

Hammer, C., "Land Sales in Eighth- and Ninth-Century Bavaria: Legal, Economic and Social Aspects", *Early Medieval Europe*, vol.6 (1997), pp.47-76.

Hammer, C., "*Lex scripta* in Early Medieval Bavaria: Use and Abuse of the *Lex Baiuvariorum*", in *Law in Mediaeval Life and Thought*, ed.E.B.King and S.J.Ridyard, Sewanee Mediaeval Studies, Nr 5 (Sewanee, 1990), pp.185-95.

Hanfmann, G.M.A., *The Season Sarcophagus in Dumbarton Oaks*, 2 vols. (Cambridge, Mass., 1951).

Heger, N., *Salzburg in römischer Zeit*, Salzburger Museum Carolino Augusteum, Jahreschrift 1973-19 (Salzburg, 1974).

Henisch, B.A., "In Due Season: Farm Work in the Medieval Calendar Tradition", in *Agriculture in the Middle Ages; Technology, Practice and Representation*, ed.D.Sweeney (Philadelphia, 1995), pp.309-36.

Herrschaft, Kirche, Kultur. Beiträge zur Geschichte des Mittelalters. Festschrift für Friedrich Prinz zu seinem 65.Geburtstag, ed.G.Jenal and S.Haarländer, Monographien zur Geschichte des Mittelalters, vol.37 (Stuttgart, 1993).

Jahn, J., *Ducatus Baiuvariorum. Das Bairische Herzogtum der Agilolfinger*, Monographien zur Geschichte des Mittelalters, vol.35 (Stuttgart, 1991).

Jarnut, J., *Agilolfingerstudien. Untersuchungen zur Geschichte einer adligen Familie im 6.und 7.Jahrhundert*, Monographien zur Geschichte des Mittelalters, vol.32 (Stuttgart, 1986).

Jarnut, J., "Genealogie und politische Bedeutung der agilolfingischen Herzöge", *Mitteilungen des Instituts für österreichische Geschichtsforschung*, vol.99 (1991), pp.1-22.

Jarnut, J., *Prosopographische und sozialgeschichtliche Studien zum Langobardenreich in Italien (568-774)*, Bonner Historische Forschungen, vol.38 (Bonn, 1972).

Jarnut, J., "Untersuchungen zu den fränkisch-alemannischen Beziehungen in der ersten Hälfte des 8. Jahrhunderts", *Schweizerische Zeitschrift für Geschichte*, vol.30 (1980), pp.7-28.

Jobst, W., *Römische Mosaiken in Salzburg* (Vienna, 1982).

Jones, C.W., "An Early Medieval Licensing Examination", *History of Education Quarterly*, vol.3 (1963), pp.19-29.

Kantorowicz, E.H., *Laudes Regiae; A Study in Liturgical Acclamations and Medieval Ruler Worship*, University of California Publications in History, vol.33 (Berkeley & Los Angeles, 1946).

Karl der Grosse und die Wissenschaft, ed.E.Irblich with a contribution from H.Wolfram (Vienna, 1994).

Karl der Große. Lebenswerk und Nachleben, vol.1 (Persönlichkeit und Geschichte), ed.H.Beumann; vol.2 (Das Geistige Leben), ed.B.Bischoff; vol.3 (Karolingische Kunst), ed.W.Braunfels and H.Schnitzler (Düsseldorf, 1965).

Kenner, H., "Römische Mosaiken aus Österreich", in *La mosaïque gréco-romaine*, (Paris, 1965), pp.85-94 + Plates.

Klibansky, R., E.Panofsky and F.Saxl, *Saturn and Melancholy; Studies in the History of Natural Philosophy, Religion and Art* (London, 1964).

Kottje, R., "Die Lex Baiuvariorum-das Recht der Baiern", in *Überlieferung und Geltung normativer Texte des frühen und hohen Mittelalters*, ed.H.Mordek, Quellen und Forschungen zum Recht im Mittelalter, vol.4 (Sigmaringen, 1986), pp.9-23.

Bibliography

Kuchenbuch, L., *Bäuerliche Gesellschaft und Klosterherrschaft im 9.Jahrhundert. Studien zur Sozialstruktur der Familia der Abtei Prüm*, Vierteljahrschrift für Sozial- und Wirtschaftsgeschichte, Beiheft Nr 66 (Wiesbaden, 1978).

Laske, W., "Die Mönchung Herzog Tassilos III. und das Schicksal seiner Angehörigen", in *Die Anfänge des Klosters Kremsmünster*, ed.S.Haider, Mitteilungen des Oberösterreichischen Landesarchivs, Ergänzungsband 2 (Linz, 1978), pp.189-97.

Lohrmann, D., "Alcuins Korrespondenz mit Karl dem Großen über Kalendar und Astronomie", in *Science in Western and Eastern Civilization*, pp.79-114.

MacCormack, S., *Art and Ceremony in Late Antiquity* (Berkeley, 1981).

Mane, P., "Du livre-cathédrale au livre d'heures: le calendrier et les travaux des mois", in *Paysages, paysans. L'art et la terre en Europe du Moyen âge au XXe siècle* (Paris, 1994).

Mayr, G., *Studien zum Adel im frühmittelalterlichen Bayern*, Studien zur bayerischen Verfassungs- und Sozialgeschichte, vol.5 (Munich, 1974).

McCluskey, S., "Astronomies in the Latin West from the Fifth to the Ninth Centuries", in *Science in Western and Eastern Civilization*, pp.139-60.

McCormick, M., "Textes, images et iconoclasme dans le cadre des relations entre Byzance et l'Occident carolingien", in *Testo e immagine*, pp.95-162.

McCulloh, J., "Martyrologium Excarpsatum: A New Text from the Early Middle Ages", in *Saints Scholars and Heroes*, pp.179-237.

McGurk, P., "Carolingian Astrological Manuscripts", in *Charles the Bald: Court and Kingdom*, ed.M.Gibson and J.Nelson, BAR International Series, vol.101 (London, 1981), pp.317-32.

Messner, D., "Salzburgs Romanen", in *Virgil von Salzburg. Missionar und Gelehrter*, ed.H.Dopsch and R.Juffinger (Salzburg, 1985), pp.103-11.

Mitterauer, M., *Karolingische Markgrafen im Südosten. Fränkische Reichsaristokratie und bayerischer Stammesadel im österreichischen Raum*, Archiv für österreichische Geschichte, vol.123 (Vienna, 1963).

Nees, L., "Carolingian Art and Politics", in *"The Gentle Voices of Teachers"*, pp.186-226.

Nees, L., *A Tainted Mantle; Hercules and the Classical Tradition at the Carolingian Court* (Philadelphia, 1991).

Noble, T.F.X., "Tradition and Learning in Search of Ideology: the *Libri Carolini*", in *"The Gentle Voices of Teachers"*, pp.227-60, esp.pp.246-8.

Noll, R., *Frühes Christentum in Österreich. Von den Anfängen bis um 600 nach Chr.* (Vienna, 1954)

Obrist, B., "Wind Diagrams and Medieval Cosmology", *Speculum*, vol.72 (1997), pp.33-84.

Parrish, D., *Season Mosaics of Roman North Africa*, Archaeologica 46 (Rome, 1984).

Pillinger, R., "Die malerische Innenausstattung frühchristlicher Kirchen in Noricum", in *Das Christentum im bairischen Raum von den Anfängen bis ins 11.Jahrhundert*, ed.E.Boshof and H.Wolff, Passauer historische Forschungen, vol.8 (Cologne, 1994), pp.231-40.

Platelle, H., *Le temporel de l'abbaye de Saint-Amand des origines a 1340*, Bibliothéque Elzévirienne (Paris, 1962).

Prinz, F., "Arbeo von Freising und die Agilulfinger", *Zeitschrift für bayerische Landesgeschichte*, vol.29 (1966), pp.580-90.

Raff, T., "Die Ikonographie der mittelalterlichen Windpersonifikationen", *Aachener Kunstblätter*, vol.48 (1978/9), pp.71-218.

Reindel, K., "Bayern im Karolingerreich", *Karl der Große*, vol.1, pp.220-46.

Reindel, K., "Die Errichtung einer neuen Bistumsorganisation" and "Politische Geschichte Bayerns im Karolingerreich", in *Handbuch der bayerischen Geschichte*, vol.1 (Das Alte Bayern. Das Stammesherzogtum bis zum Ausgang des 12.Jahrhunderts), ed.M.Spindler, 2nd rev.edn (Munich, 1981).

Richter, M., "Die Sprachpolitik Karls des Großen", *Sprachwissenschaft*, vol.7 (1982), pp.412-37.

Riegl, A., "Die mittelalterliche Kalenderillustration", *Mitteilungen des Instituts für österreichische Geschichtsforschung*, vol.10 (1889), pp.1-74.

Rodgers, R., *An Introduction to Palladius*, University of London, Institute of Classical Studies, Bulletin Supplement Nr 35 (London, 1975).

Ross, J.B., "Two Neglected Paladins of Charlemagne: Erich of Friuli and Gerold of Bavaria", *Speculum*, vol.20 (1945), pp.212-35.

Rück, K., *Auszüge aus der Naturgeschichte des C.Plinius Secundus in einem astronomisch-komputistischen Sammelwerke des achten Jahrhunderts*, Program des Königlichen Ludwigs-Gymnasiums für das Studienjahr 1887/88 (Munich, 1888).

Saints Scholars and Heroes; Studies in Medieval Culture in Honour of Charles W.Jones, vol.2, ed.M.H.King and W.M.Stevens (Collegeville, 1979).

Salzman, M.R., *On Roman Time; The Codex-Calendar of 354 and the Rhythms of Urban Life in Late Antiquity*, The Transformation of the Classical Heritage, vol.17 (Berkeley, 1990).

Saxl, F., *Verzeichnis astrologischer und mythologischer illustrierter Handschriften des lateinischen Mittelalters*, vol.2, Sitzungsberichte der Heidelberger Akademie der Wissenschaften, Sitzungsberichte, Phil.-hist.Klasse, 1925-26/2 (Heidelberg, 1927).

Schieffer, R., "Karl Martell und seine Familie", in *Karl Martell in seiner Zeit*, ed.J.Jarnut *et al.*, Beihefte der Francia, vol.37 (Sigmaringen, 1994), pp.305-15.

Schieffer, R., "Karolingische Töchter", in *Herrschaft, Kirche, Kultur*, pp.125-39.

Schramm, P.E., "Die Bedeutung von Zahl und Winkel für Karls Denkart", in *idem, Kaiser, Könige und Päpste. Gesammelte Aufsätze zur Geschichte des Mittelalters*, vol.1 (Beiträge zur Allgemeinen Geschichte, Pt.I) (Stuttgart, 1968).

Schramm, P.E., *Die deutschen Kaiser und Könige in Bildern ihrer Zeit., 751-1190*, rev.edn., F.Mütherich *et.al.* (Munich, 1983).

Schreibmüller, H., "Audulf, der früheste bezeugte Graf im Taubergau", *Mainfränkisches Jahrbuch*, vol.3 (1951), pp.53-69.

Schulze, H.K., *Die Grafschaftsverfassung der Karolingerzeit in den Gebieten östlich des Rheins*, Schriften zur Verfassungsgeschichte, vol.19 (Berlin, 1973).

Science in Western and Eastern Civilization in Carolingian Times, ed.P.L.Butzer & D.Lohrmann (Basel, 1993).

Slim, H., "Eternal Time and cyclical time", in *Mosaics of Roman Africa; Floor Mosaics from Tunisia*, ed. M.Blanchard-Lemée *et.al.* (New York, 1996), pp.37-64.

Staab, F., *Untersuchungen zur Gesellschaft am Mittelrhein in der Karolingerzeit*, Geschichtliche Landeskunde, vol.11 (Wiesbaden, 1975).

Staubach, N., *Rex Christianus. Hofkultur und Herrschaftspropaganda im Reich Karls des Kahlen*, Part II, Pictura et poesis, vol.2/II (Cologne/Weimar/Vienna, 1993).

Stern, H., *Le calendrier de 354. Étude sur son texte et ses illustrations*, Bibliothèque archéologique et historique, vol.55 (Paris, 1953).

Stern, H., "Les calendriers romains illustrés", *Aufstieg und Niedergang der Römischen*

Welt II (Principat), vol.12,2 (Berlin, 1981), pp.431-75.

Stern, H., "Poésies et représentations carolingiennes et byzantines des mois", *Revue Archéologique*, vol.45 (1955), pp.141-86.

Stevens, W., "*Compostistica et astronomica* in the Fulda School", in *Saints, Scholars and Heroes*, pp.27-63.

Störmer, W., "Eine Adelsgruppe um die Fuldaer Äbte Sturmi und Eigil und den Holzkirchener Klostergründer Troand. Beobachtungen zum bayerisch-alemannisch-ostfränkischen Adel des 8./9. Jahrhunderts", in *Gesellschaft und Herrschaft. Forschungen zu sozial- und landesgeschichtlichen Problemen. Festgabe zum 60.Geburtstag von Karl Bosl* (Munich, 1969), pp.1-34.

Störmer, W., *Adelsgruppen im früh- und hochmittelalterlichen Bayern*, Studien zur bayerischen Verfassungs- und Sozialgeschichte, vol.4 (Munich, 1972)

Störmer, W., "Einhards Herkunft. Überlegungen und Beobachtungen zu Einhards Erbbesitz und familiären Umfeld" (forthcoming; kindly provided to me in manuscript by the author).

Störmer, W., *Früher Adel. Studien zur politischen Führungsschicht im fränkisch-deutschen Reich vom 8.bis 11.Jahrhundert*, 2 Parts, Monographien zur Geschichte des Mittelalters, vol.6 (Stuttgart, 1973).

Störmer, W., "Das Herzogsgeschlecht der Agilolfinger", in *Die Bajuwaren*, pp.141-52.

Sturm, J., *Die Anfänge des Hauses Preysing*, Schriftenreihe zur bayerischen Landesgeschichte, vol.8, (Munich, 1931, reprint 1974).

Swarzenski, G., *Die Salzburger Malerei. Von den Ersten Anfängen bis zur Blütezeit des romanischen Stils*, Studien zur Geschichte der deutschen Malerei und Handschriftenkunde des Mittelalters, Textband/Tafelband (Leipzig, 1913/1908).

Tellenbach, G., *Königtum und Stämme in der Werdezeit des Deutschen Reiches*, Quellen und Studien zur Verfassungsgeschichte des Deutschen Reiches in Mittelalter und Neuzeit, vol.7/4 (Weimar, 1939).

Testo e immagine nell'alto medioevo, Settimane di Studio, vol.41,1 (Spoleto, 1994).

Tremp, E., *Studien zu den Gesta Hludowici imperatoris des Trierer Chorbischofs Thegan*, Schriften der MGH, vol.32 (Hannover, 1988).

Van Der Meer, F., *Maiestas Domini. Théophanies de l'apocalypse dans l'art chrétien*, Studi di Antichità Cristiana, vol.13 (Vatican City, 1938).

Viellard-Troiekouroff, M., "Nouvelles études sur les mosaïques de Germigny-des-Prés", *Cahiers archéologiques*, vol.17 (1967), pp.104-12.

Un village au temps de Charlemagne. Moines et paysans de l'abbaye de Saint-Denis du VIIe siècle à l'An Mil (Paris, 1988).

Wagner, N., "Zur Herkunft der Agilolfinger", *Zeitschrift für bayerische Landesgeschichte*, vol.41 (1978), pp.19-48.

Wallach, L., *Diplomatic Studies in Latin and Greek Documents from the Carolingian Age* (Ithaca, 1977).

Wallis, F., "Images of Order in the Medieval Computus", in *Ideas of Order in the Middle Ages*, ed.W.Ginsberg, Acta of the Center for Medieval and Early Renaissance Studies, vol.15 (Binghampton, 1990), pp.45-68.

Wavra, B., *Salzburg und Hamburg. Erzbistumsgründung und Missionspolitik in karolingischer Zeit*, Giessener Abhandlungen zur Agrar- und Wirtschaftsforschung des europäischen Ostens, vol.179 (Berlin, 1991).

Webster, J.C., *The Labors of the Months in Antique and Medieval Art to the End of the Twelfth Century*, Princeton Monographs in Art and Archaeology, vol.21 (Princeton, 1938).

Wenskus, R., *Sächsischer Stammesadel und fränkischer Reichsadel*, Abhandlungen der Akademie der Wissenschaften in Göttingen,

Phil.-hist.Kl., 3.Folge, Nr 93 (Göttingen, 1976).

Werner, K.F., "Bedeutende Adelsfamilien im Reich Karls des Großen", *Karl der Große*, vol.1, pp.83-142.

White, K.D., *Agricultural Implements of the Roman World* (Cambridge, 1967).

White, K.D., *Farm Equipment of the Roman World* (Cambridge, 1975).

White, L., *Medieval Technology and Social Change* (Oxford, 1962).

Wisplinghoff, E., "Hildebald", in *Neue Deutsche Biographie*, vol.9 (Berlin, 1972), p.118.

Wolfram, H., *Die Geburt Mitteleuropas. Geschichte Österreichs vor seiner Enstehung* (Vienna, 1987).

Wolfram, H., *Salzburg, Bayern, Österreich. Die Conversio Bagoariorum et Carantanorum und die Quellen ihrer Zeit*, Mitteilungen des Instituts für österreichische Geschichtsforschung, Suppl., vol.31 (Vienna, 1995).

Wormald, F., *The Utrecht Psalter* (Utrecht, 1953).

Zöllner, E., "Die Herkunft der Agilulfinger", in *Zur Geschichte der Bayern*, ed.K.Bosl, Wege der Forschung, vol.60 (Darmstadt, 1965), pp.107-34 (reprinted from *Mitteilungen des Instituts für österreichische Geschichtsforschung*, vol.59 [1951], pp.245-64).

Addendum

After completing the manuscript, the following study came to my notice:

Achilles, W., "Der Monatsbilderzyklus zweier Salzburger Handschriften des frühen 9. Jahrhunderts in agrarhistorischer Sicht", in *Theorie und Empirie in Wirtschaftspolitik und Wirtschaftsgeschichte. Festschrift für Wilhelm Abel zum 80.Geburtstag*, ed.K.H.Kaufhold and F.Riemann, Göttinger Beiträge zur Wirtschafts- und Sozialgeschichte, vol.11 (Göttingen, 1984), pp.85-107.

Professor Achilles, a well-known historian of early-modern agriculture, uses sources from his period to interpret the pictures, and confines his examination to the months beginning in June. He concludes, as do I, that the order of the labors, June-October, represents a specifically "German" sequence of agricultural tasks (esp.pp.98-106). He also adduces some interesting arguments for considering the combined representation of November-December as a hunting scene rather than pasturage on the mast and domestic slaughter (pp.90-1).

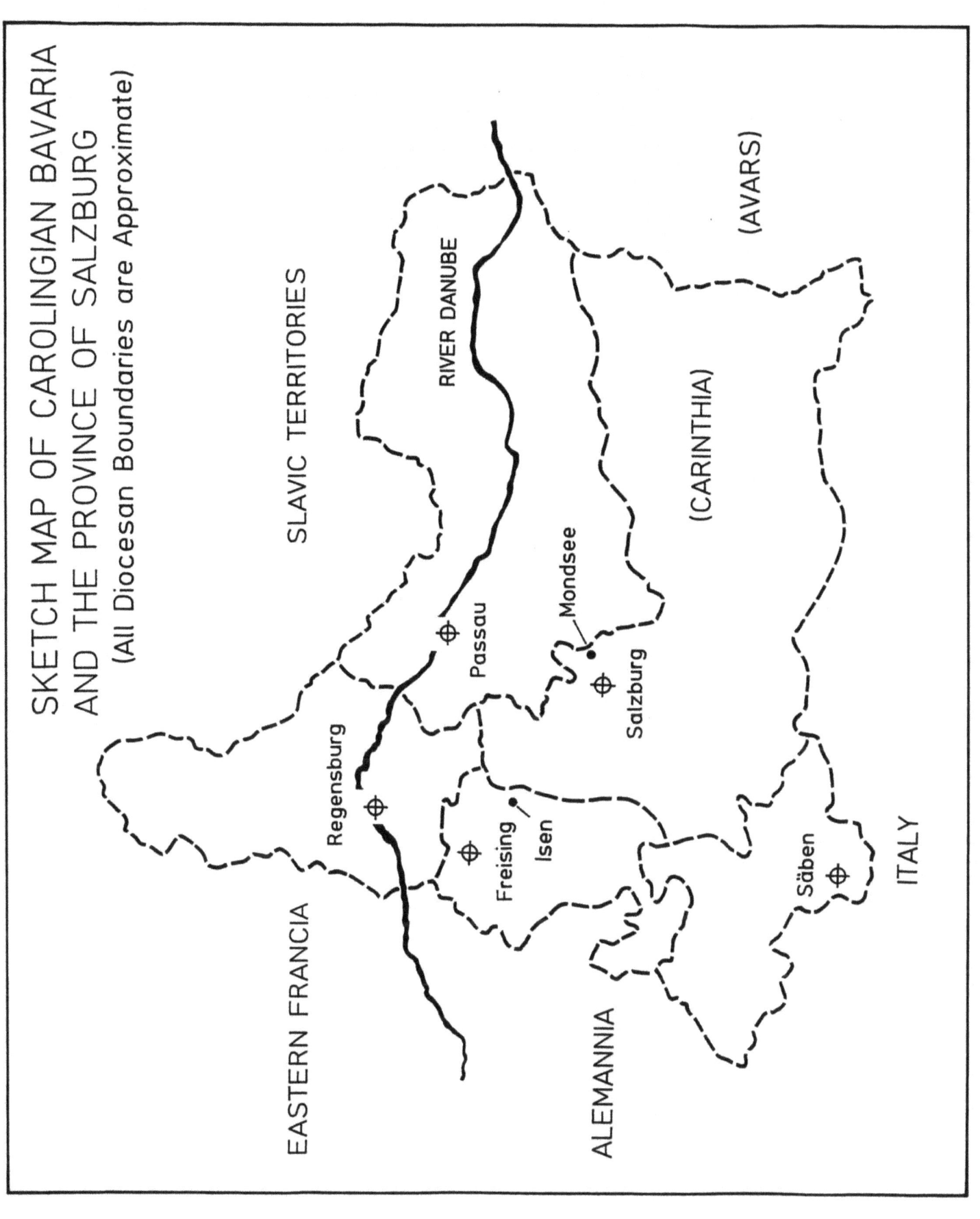

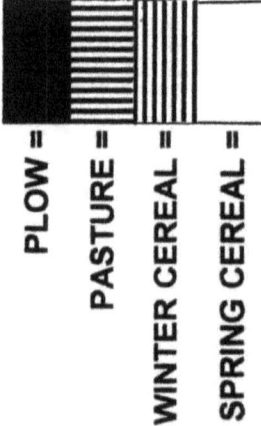

Exhibit
Typology of Classical and Medieval Seasonal Representations

	Classical	**Medieval**
Dominant Periodical Division	4 Seasons	12 Months
Type of Representation	Personification with Attribute	Genre Scene
Agricultural Activities	Multiple/Period	One/Period
Pose of Figures	Passive	Active
Religious Festivals	Included	Absent
Manuscript Context	Secular	Religious

TABLE 1
COMPARISON OF CLASSICAL AND MEDIEVAL LABORS OF THE MONTHS

MONTH	MENOLOGIA RUSTICA (1st cent)	ST ROMAIN-EN-GAL MOSAIC (2nd/3rd cent)	ROMAN CODEX-CALENDAR (354)	CHARLEMAGNE'S NAME FOR MONTH (after 800)	SALZBURG MANUSCRIPT (by 818)	WANDALBERT OF PRÜM MENSIUM XII DESCRIPTIO (848)	WANDALBERT OF PRÜM MARTYROLOGY (later 9th cent)	GERMANY (5x) (late 10th-12th cent)	FRANCE (17x) (12th cent)
JAN	1) SHARPEN STAKES 2) CUT WILLOWS & REEDS	WI: BAKE BREAD WI: SACRIFICE TO LARES WI: CUT REEDS & WEAVE BASKETS	MAN IN LONG TUNIC MAKING OFFERING IN BURNING BRAZIER; ROOSTER	WINTER	MAN WARMING	1) FOWLING 2) CUT WOOD FOR BUILDINGS & BOATS	PIG SLAUGHTER /FEASTING ?	FEASTING (2) JANUS FIGURE (2) HUNTING HARES (1)	FEASTING (9)
FEB	1) HOE CORNFIELD 2) CULTIVATE VINES 3) BURN OFF REEDS	WI: FEAST OF PARENTALIA	WOMAN IN LONG, HOODED ROBE HOLDING WATERFOWL; WATER POURING FROM VASE, FISH, SEA CREATURES	"HORNUNG" ("BASTARD"/"SHORT"?)	FOWLING (WATERFOWL ?)	1) BREAK UP FIELDS 2) SOW BARLEY 3) PRUNE VINES 4) HUNT LARGE GAME 5) SET UP FISH WEIRS	MAN WARMING	WOOD CUTTING (4 ?) NIL (1)	MAN WARMING (15)
MAR	1) PRUNE & TRENCH VINES 2) SOW SPRING WHEAT	SP: STORKS ARRIVE SP: GRAFT TREES	MAN IN SKIN TUNIC WITH GOAT, BIRDS, BUCKET	SPRING	MAN WITH SMALL BIRD & SNAKE	1) FENCE & DUNG FIELDS 2) SOW VARIOUS CROPS 3) PREPARE BEEHIVES 4) REPLANT ORCHARDS 5) GRAFT TREES	FISHES (ZODIAC ?)	PRUNING (3) DIGGING (1) FIGURE WITH BASKET & VINE (1)	PRUNING (14)
APR	WASH SHEEP		MAN IN SHORT TUNIC DANCING WITH RATTLES; STATUE OF GODDESS	EASTER	PRUNING/GRAFTING; CUTTING LEAF BUDS FOR FODDER ?	1) TURN OUT STALLED ANIMALS TO GRAZE 2) DITCH & FENCE FIELDS 3) FLOOD PASTURES 4) TIE & PROP VINES	MAN WITH SPROUTS	FLOWER-BEARER (3) DIGGING (1) VINE CULTURE (1)	FLOWER-BEARER (10)
MAY	1) WEED CORNFIELD 2) SHEAR SHEEP 3) WASH WOOL 4) TAME BULLOCKS 5) CUT FODDER 6) CLEAN CORNFIELD		MAN IN LONG ROBE WITH FLOWER BASKET; PEACOCK	PASTURE	FLOWER-BEARER	1) PICK STRAWBERRIES 2) TURN UP AUTUMN-SOWN FIELDS 3) BREED LARGE ANIMALS	FLOWER-BEARER	HUNTING BIRDS (1) VINE CULTURE (1) MUSIC MAKING (1) MAN BETWEEN TREES IN LEAF (1) FLOWER-BEARER ? (1)	RIDER (14)
JUN	1) MOW HAY 2) BREAK UP VINEYARDS	SU: SACRIFICE TO JUPITER	NUDE MAN TURNED AWAY WITH TORCH; SICKLE, FRUIT BASKET, FLOWERING PLANT	FALLOW	PLOWING	1) TRANSPLANT CABBAGE 2) CUT FLOWERS 3) PICK GARDEN VEGETABLES, HERBS & FRUIT 4) MOW HAY IN PASTURES	MIDSUMMER	PLOWING (2) MOWING HAY (1) WEEDING/TILLING ? (1) UNIDENTIFIED FIGURE (1)	MOWING HAY (14)

TABLE 1
COMPARISON OF CLASSICAL AND MEDIEVAL LABORS OF THE MONTHS

MONTH	MENOLOGIA RUSTICA (1st cent)	ST ROMAIN-EN-GAL MOSAIC (2nd/3rd cent)	ROMAN CODEX-CALENDAR (354)	CHARLEMAGNE'S NAME FOR MONTH (after 800)	SALZBURG MANUSCRIPT (by 818)	WANDALBERT OF PRÜM MENSIUM XII DESCRIPTIO (848)	WANDALBERT OF PRÜM MARTYROLOGY (later 9th cent)	GERMANY (5x) (late 10th-12th cent)	FRANCE (17x) (12th cent)
J U L	1) HARVEST BARLEY 2) BEGIN WHEAT HARVEST	SU: HARVEST FESTIVAL	NUDE MAN HOLDING PURSE AND BASKET WITH PLANTS; COINS, COVERED CONTAINERS	HAY	MOWER	1) BEGIN WHEAT, SPELT HARVEST 2) PICK FRUIT 3) HUNT STAGS	MOWING HAY	MOWING HAY (4) REAPING GRAIN (1)	REAPING GRAIN (13)
A U G	1) FINISH WHEAT HARVEST 2) PREPARE STAKES 3) THRESH GRAIN 4) BURN OFF STUBBLE	SU: CUT STRAW	NUDE MAN DRINKING FROM BOWL; HUNG JACKET, FAN, MELONS, AMPHORA	HARVEST	REAPING GRAIN	1) MAIN HARVEST OF SPELT, OATS, BARLEY, FLAX & PULSES 2) PICK FRUIT & NUTS	REAPING GRAIN	REAPING GRAIN/HARVEST (5)	THRESHING GRAIN (13)
S E P	1) PITCH WINE JARS 2) PICK FRUIT 3) DIG UP AROUND TREES	AU: PICK FRUIT	MAN DRAPED IN LIGHT CLOTH HOLDING BASKET AND LIZARD ON STRING; GRAPE CLUSTERS, FIGS, CONTAINERS	WOOD	SOWING GRAIN	1) POST GUARDS IN VINEYARDS 2) VINTAGE OF MATURE GRAPES 3) PICK & DRY APPLES 4) SOW SPELT 5) HUNT STAGS	(MISSING)	VINTAGE: PICK GRAPES (1) TREAD GRAPES (1) MAN WITH VINES (2) SOWING GRAIN (1)	VINTAGE: TREAD GRAPES (9)
O C T	VINTAGE	AU: PICK GRAPES AU: TREAD GRAPES	MAN WITH MANTLE OVER LEFT SHOULDER HOLDING BASKET, TRAP AND HARE; HUNTING EQUIPMENT, BASKETS	VINTAGE	VINTAGE: PICKING GRAPES & PLACING IN VAT	1) MAIN VINTAGE 2) PANNAGE BEGINS 3) HUNT BOARS	VINTAGE	SOWING GRAIN (2) VINTAGE: PICK GRAPES (1) UNIDENTIFIED FIGURE (1) NIL (1)	PIG PANNAGE (8)
N O V	1) SOW WHEAT 2) SOW BARLEY 3) DITCH TREES	AU: PLOW & SOW AU: PITCH WINE (OLIVE?) JARS	MAN IN LONG TUNIC HOLDING RATTLE AND PLATTER WITH SNAKE; GOOSE, HEAD OF ANUBIS	AUTUMN	PANNAGE ?	1) SOW FIELDS 2) PANNAGE	MAN DRINKING	WOOD CUTTING (2) THRESHING GRAIN (1) OX SLAUGHTER (1) NIL (1)	PIG SLAUGHTER (8) FEED OXEN (6)
D E C	1) MANURE VINES 2) SOW BEANS 3) CUT TIMBER 4) HARVEST OLIVES 5) GO HUNTING	AU: PICK OLIVES AU: PRESS GRAPES (OLIVES?) WI: SOW BEANS WI: GRIND GRAIN WI: CARRY MANURE TO VINES	MAN IN SHORT TUNIC WITH TORCH AT DICE TABLE; BIRDS, MASK	HOLY	PIG SLAUGHTER	1) BREAK UP FIELDS 2) SPREAD DUNG 3) INDOOR TASKS 4) WATERFOWLING 5) TAKE FISH IN WEIRS 6) SLAUGHTER, SALT & SMOKE PIGS	MAN WARMING	PIG SLAUGHTER (3) FOWLING (1) NIL (1)	FEASTING (11)

85

TABLE 2
SUMMARY OF CORRESPONDENCES TO THE SALZBURG LABORS

MONTH	ROMAN CODEX-CALENDAR (354)	OTHER CLASSICAL SOURCES	LIBRI CAROLINI (790-792)	CHARLEMAGNE'S NAME FOR MONTH (after 800)
JAN	X		X	?
FEB	X		X	
MAR		?		?
APR		?		
MAY	X		X	
JUN		X		X
JUL		?		X
AUG				X
SEP		?		
OCT	X		X	X
NOV		?		?
DEC		?		

X = PROBABLE / ? = POSSIBLE

Plate 1. The Salzburg 'Labors of the Months' in Vienna, National Library, Codex 387, fo.90v.

Plate 2. Representations of February, March, August and September in the Codex-Calendar of 354, Bibliothèque Royale, Brussels

Plate 3. Representations of the Four Seasons and the Twelve Months from El Djem mosaic, Tunisia.

Plate 4. Representations of 'The Labors of the Months' in Vienna, National Library, Codex 387, fo.90v, and Munich, State Library, Clm 210, fo.91v.

Plate 5. Representations of the Winds in Vienna, National Library, Codex 387, fo.140r, and Munich, State Library, Clm 210, fo.139r.

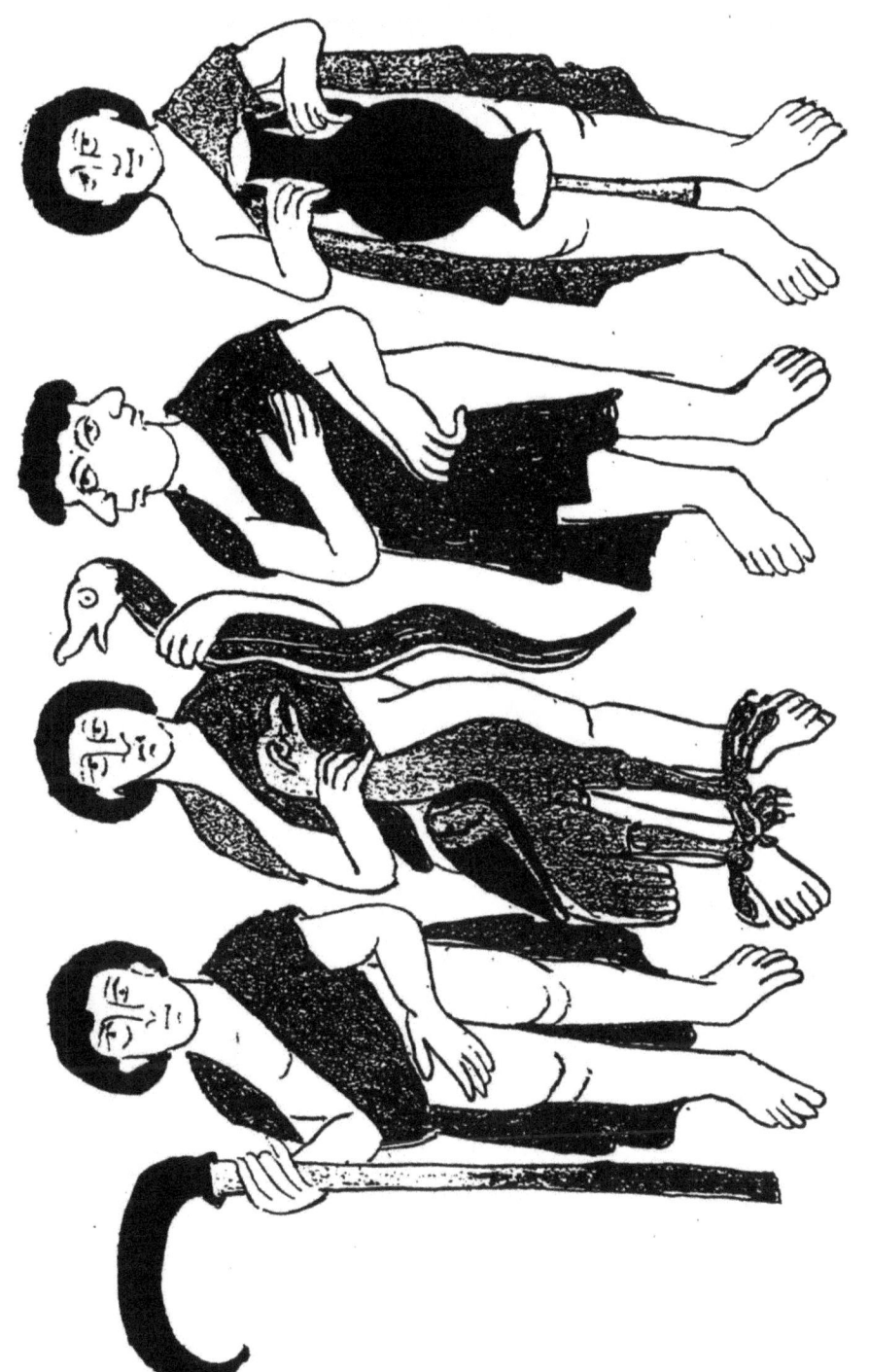

Plate 6. Representation of Jupiter in the 11th-century Montecassino Manuscript of Hrabanus Maurus' *Encyclopedia*.

91

Plate 7. Representations of the Twelve Months in the Martyrology of Wandalbert of Prüm, Vatican Library, Rome.

www.ingramcontent.com/pod-product-compliance
Lightning Source LLC
Chambersburg PA
CBHW061547010526
44114CB00027B/2954